Big Sailor

My First Big ABC

Ages 3-5

Vol.10 A-Z

  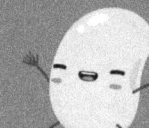  

From A to Z Recap
More Coloring Pages

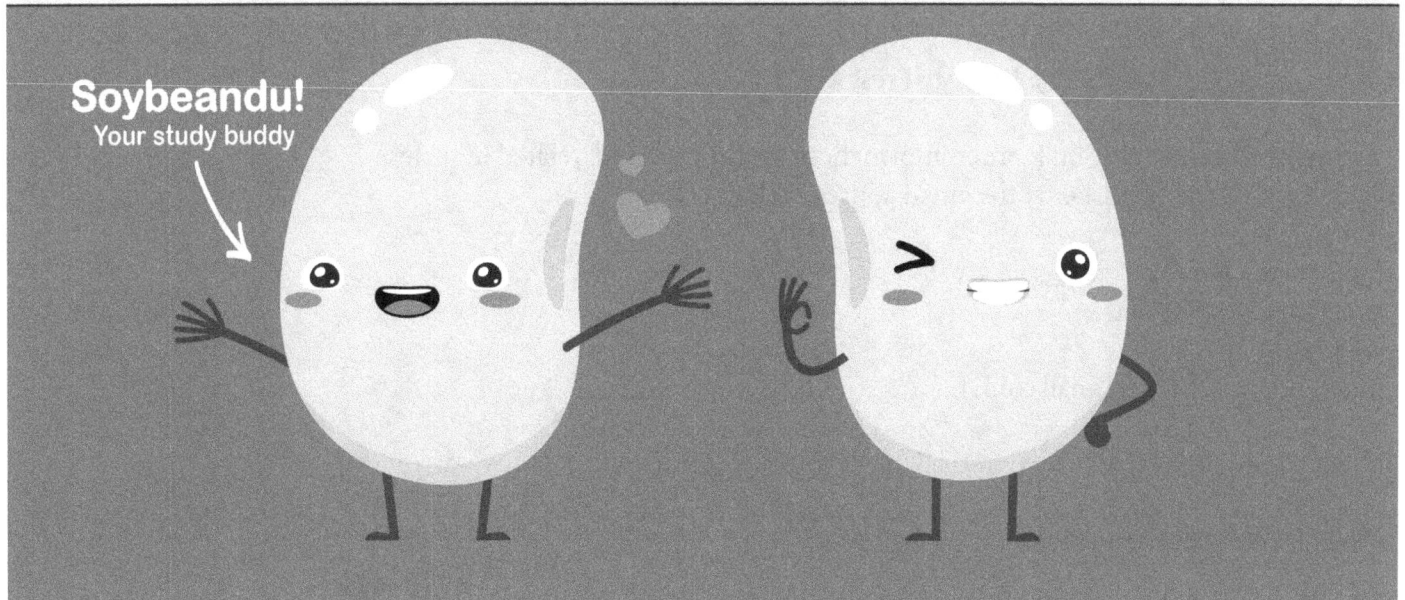

Soybeandu! Your study buddy

My First Big ABC Book Series
Big Sailor Edu

Copyright © 2021 Cambridge Dynasty Press

For permission requests, bulk order information, or any busine ss related inquries, please contact the publisher at the email address below.

Cambridge Dynasty Press
30 N Gould St. STE4000
Sheridan, WY 82801
Email: Bestsailoredu@Gmail.com

Written, Designed, and Printed in the United States of America

978-1-955650-02-1(Paperback)

47678459

Hi! Nice to meet you. My name is Soybeandu!

I am your study buddy for this book!

① Building Skills for Pen Control
② Recognizing Alphabet Letters
③ Building Confidence
④ Enjoying a Good Book
⑤ Being Patient with Practice
⑥ Developing Creative Thinking
⑦ Being Proud of Achievement
⑧ Having Fun

This book belongs to

_____
(name)

Trace the dotted line and read out loud

Trace the dotted line and read out loud

Trace the dotted line and read out loud

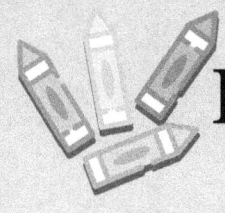 # Find the same letters and color them

Soybeandu

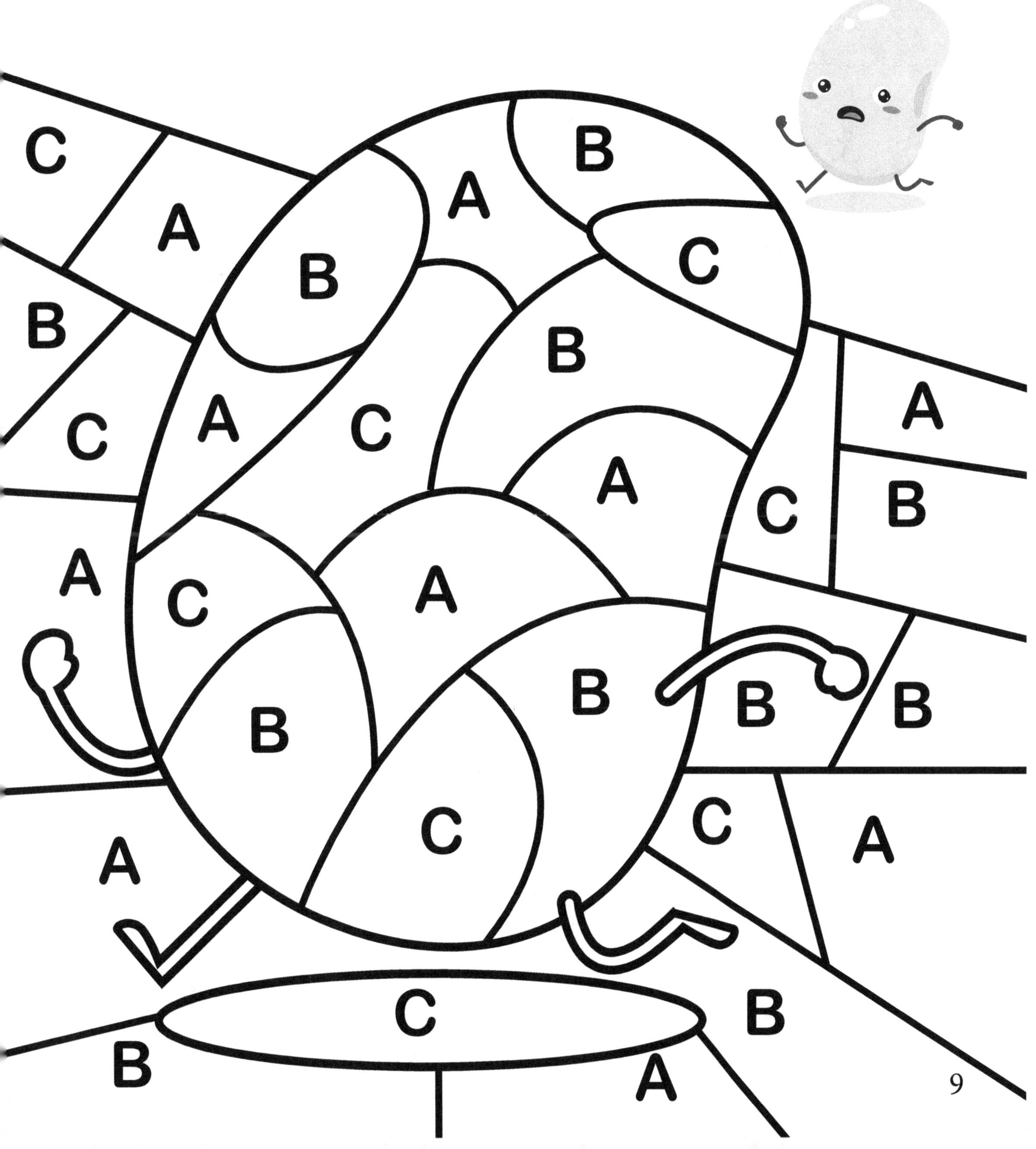

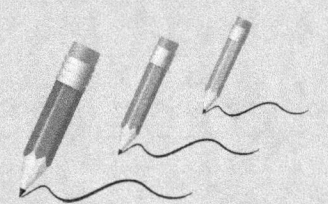
Draw lines to match

A    B    C

c   b    a

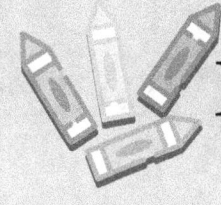 # Find the same letters and color them

Soybeandu

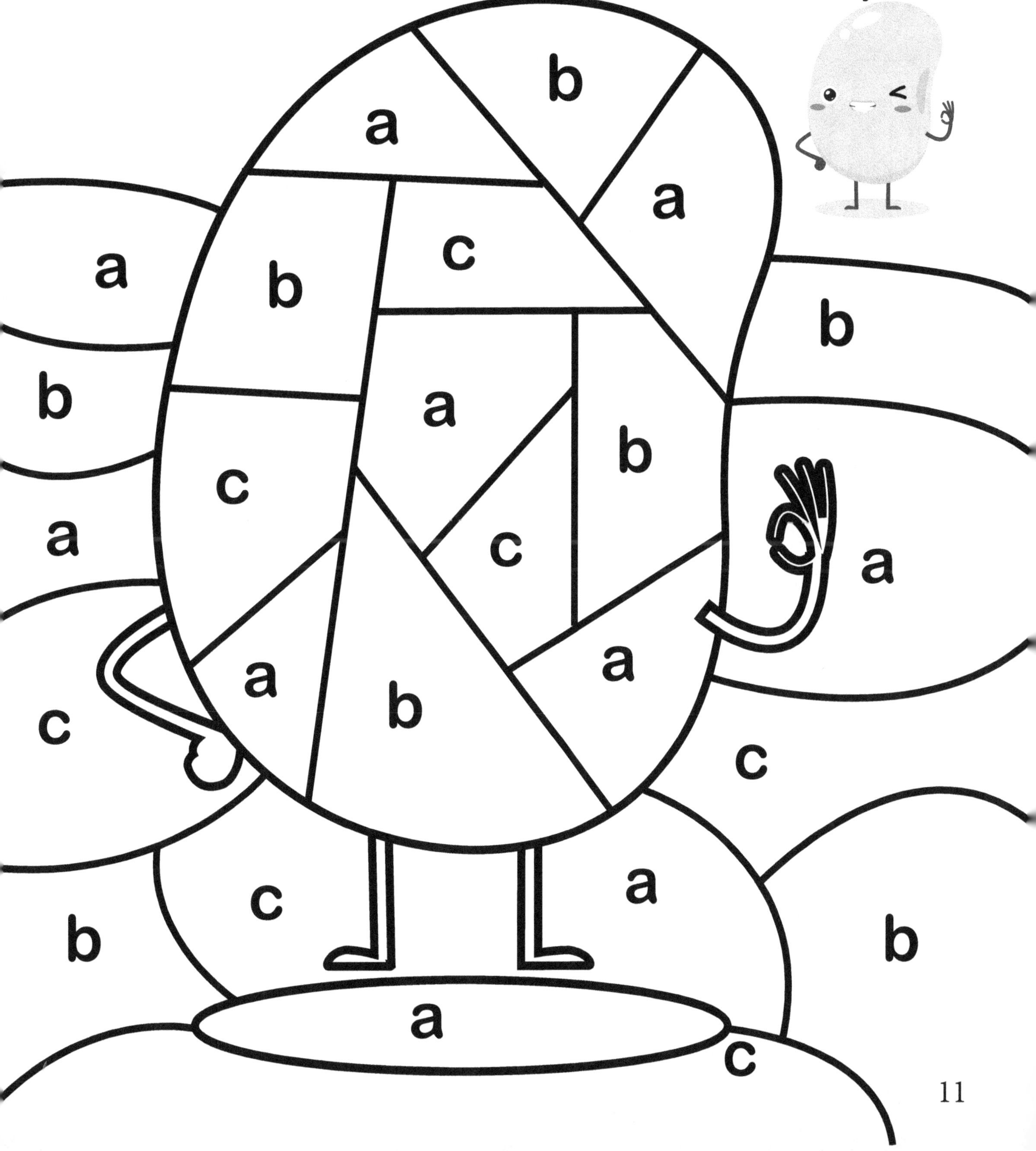

Trace the dotted line and read out loud

Trace the dotted line and read out loud

Trace the dotted line and read out loud

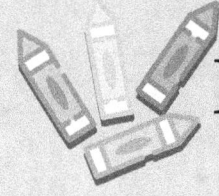 **Find the same letters and color them**

Soybeandu

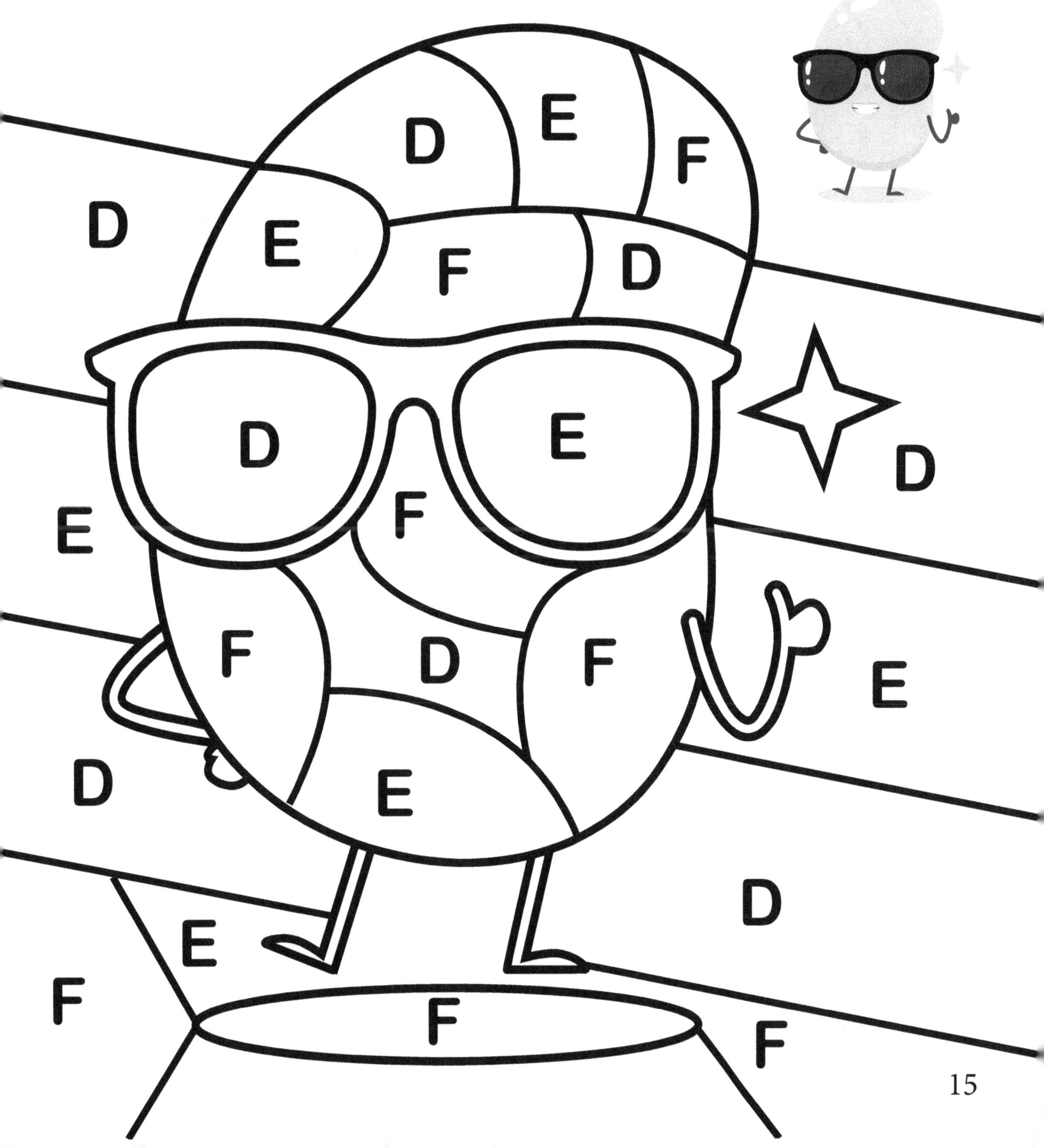

Draw lines to match

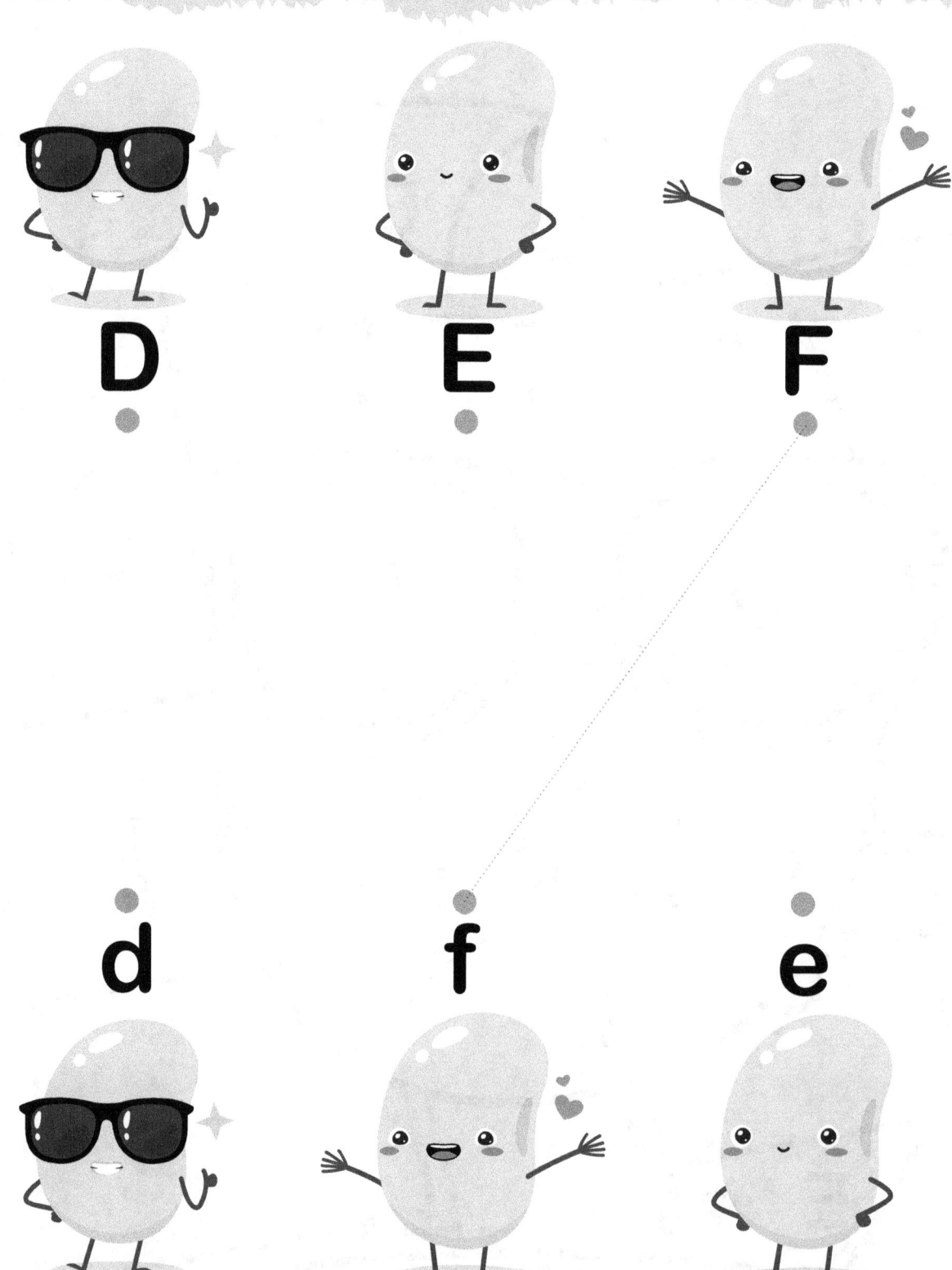

16

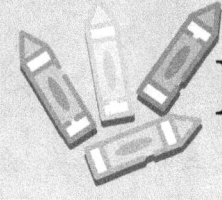 **Find the same letters and color them**

Soybeandu

Where is Soybeandu?

Find and circle!

Trace the dotted line and read out loud

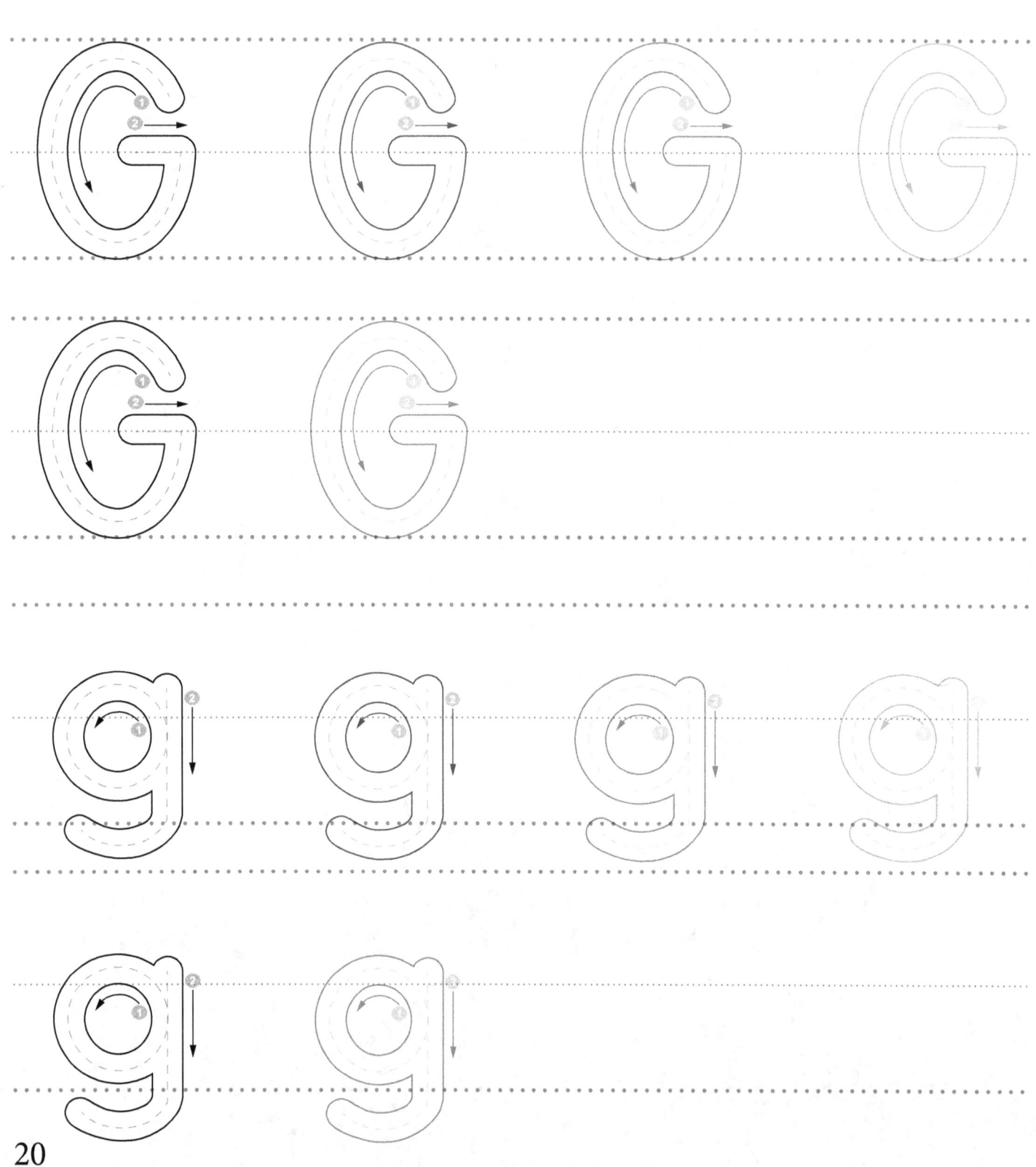

Trace the dotted line and read out loud

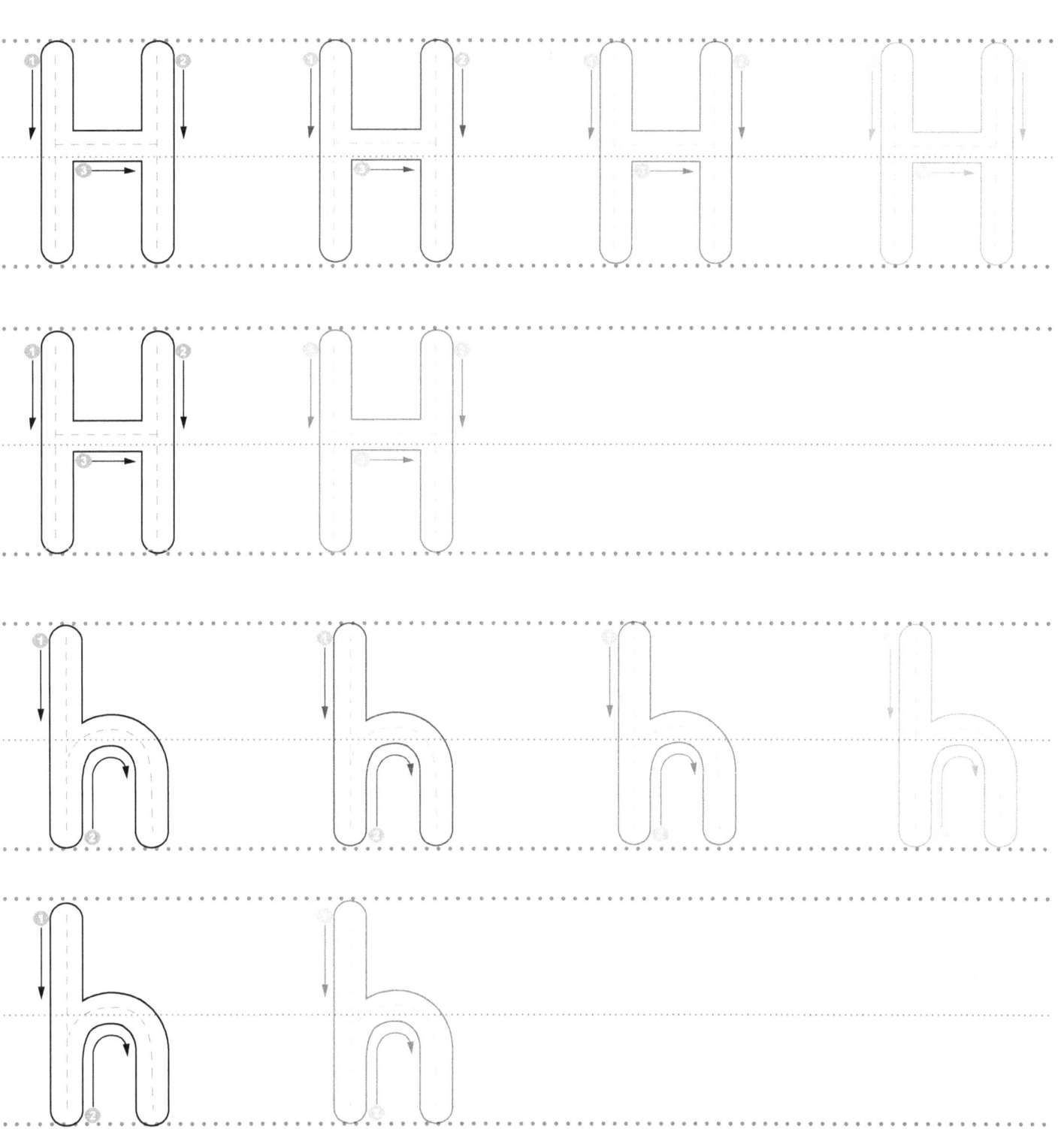

Trace the dotted line and read out loud

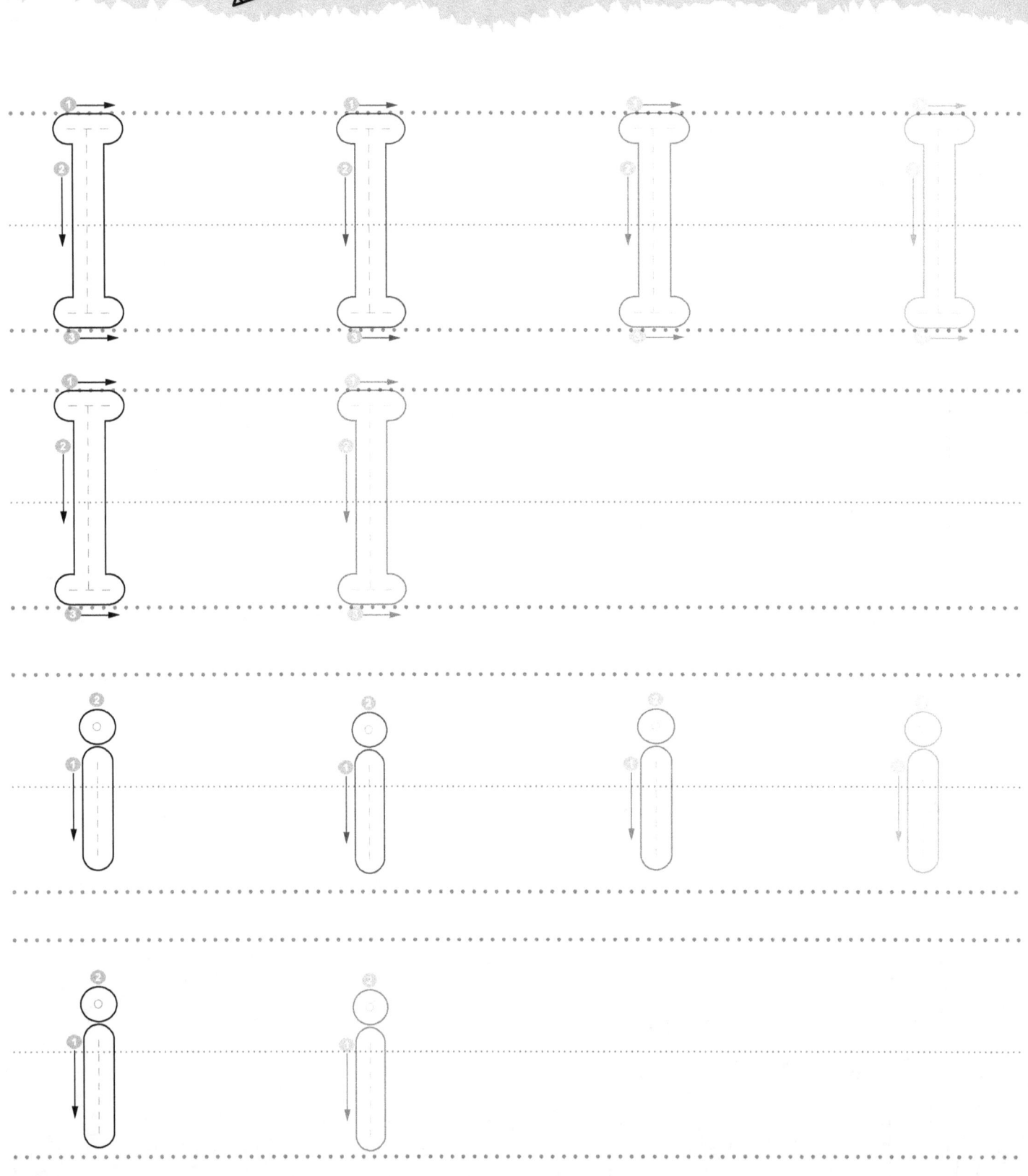

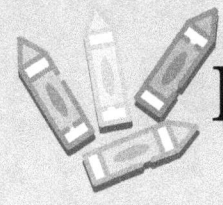 # Find the same letters and color them

Soybeandu

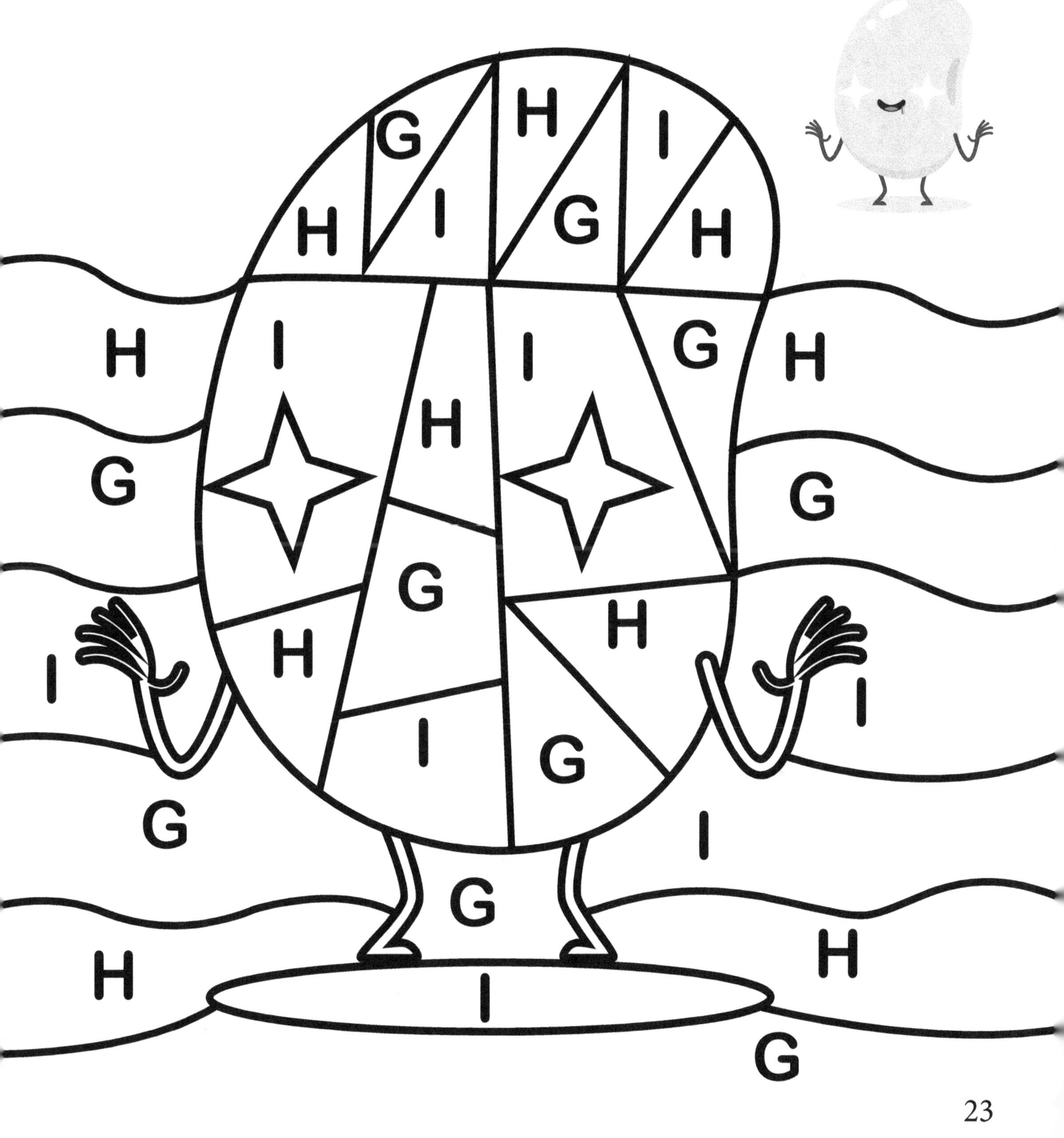

Draw lines to match

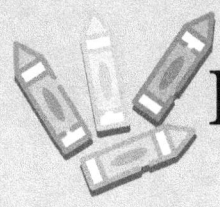 # Find the same letters and color them

Soybeandu

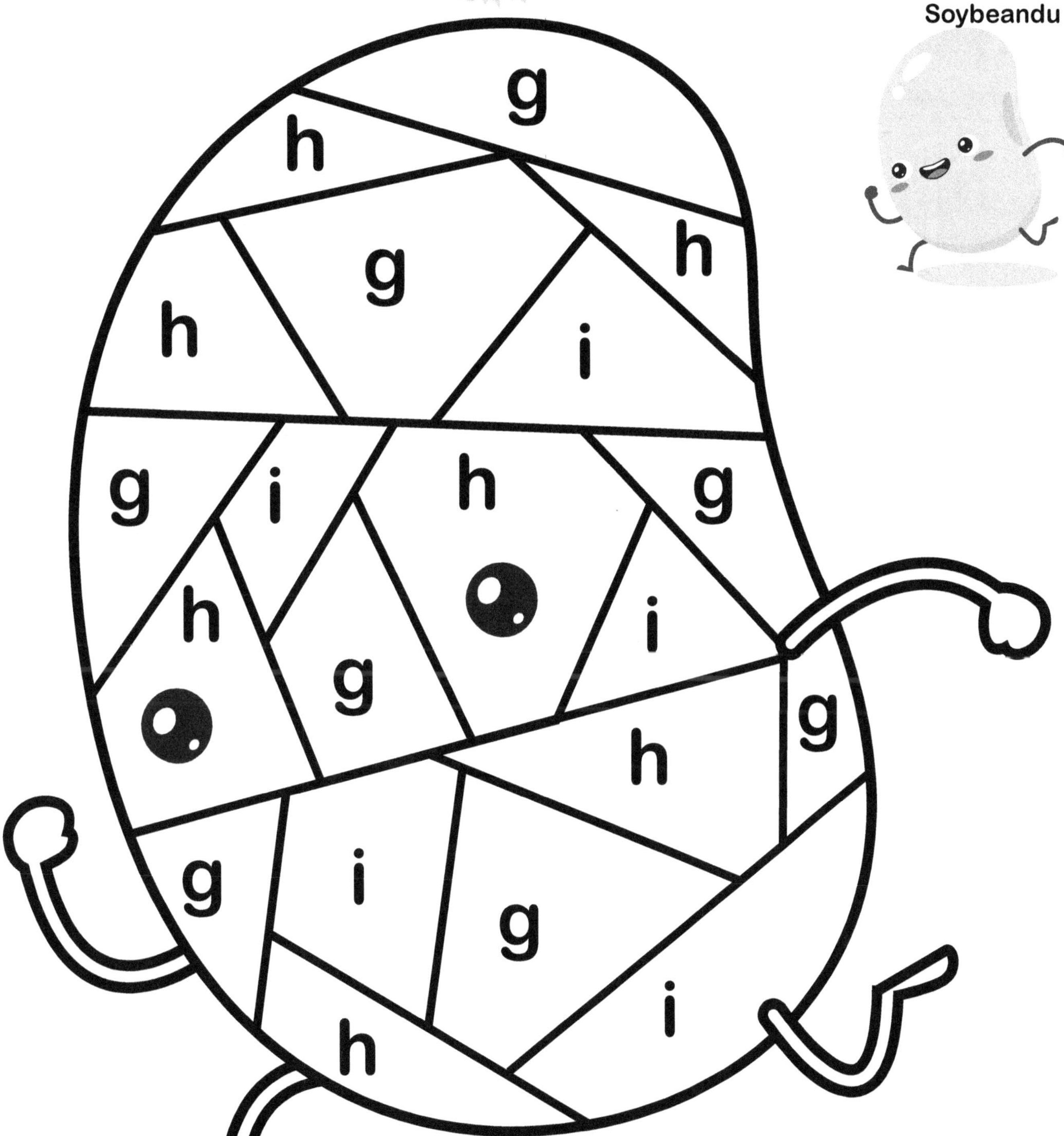

Trace the dotted line and read out loud

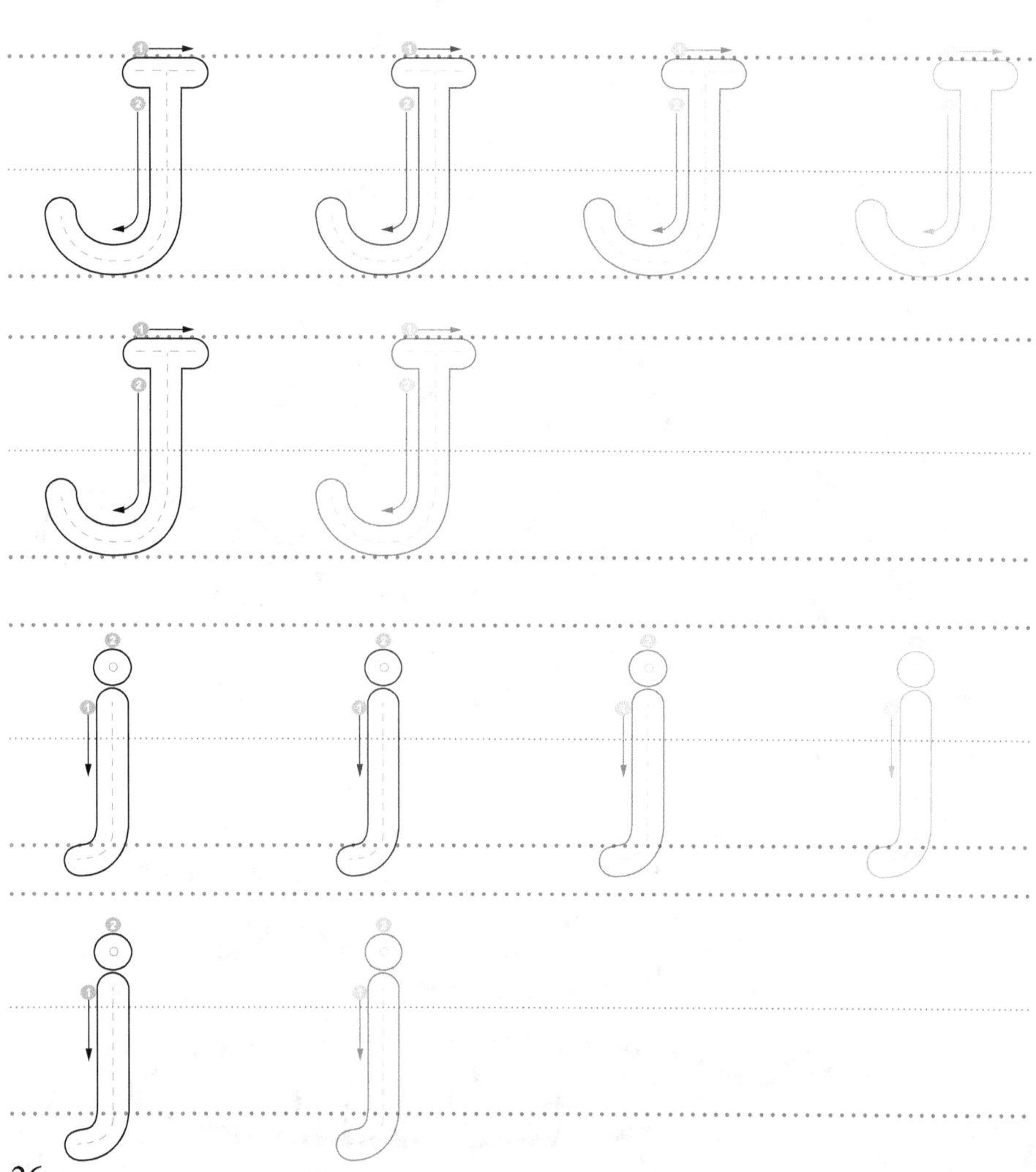

Trace the dotted line and read out loud

Trace the dotted line and read out loud

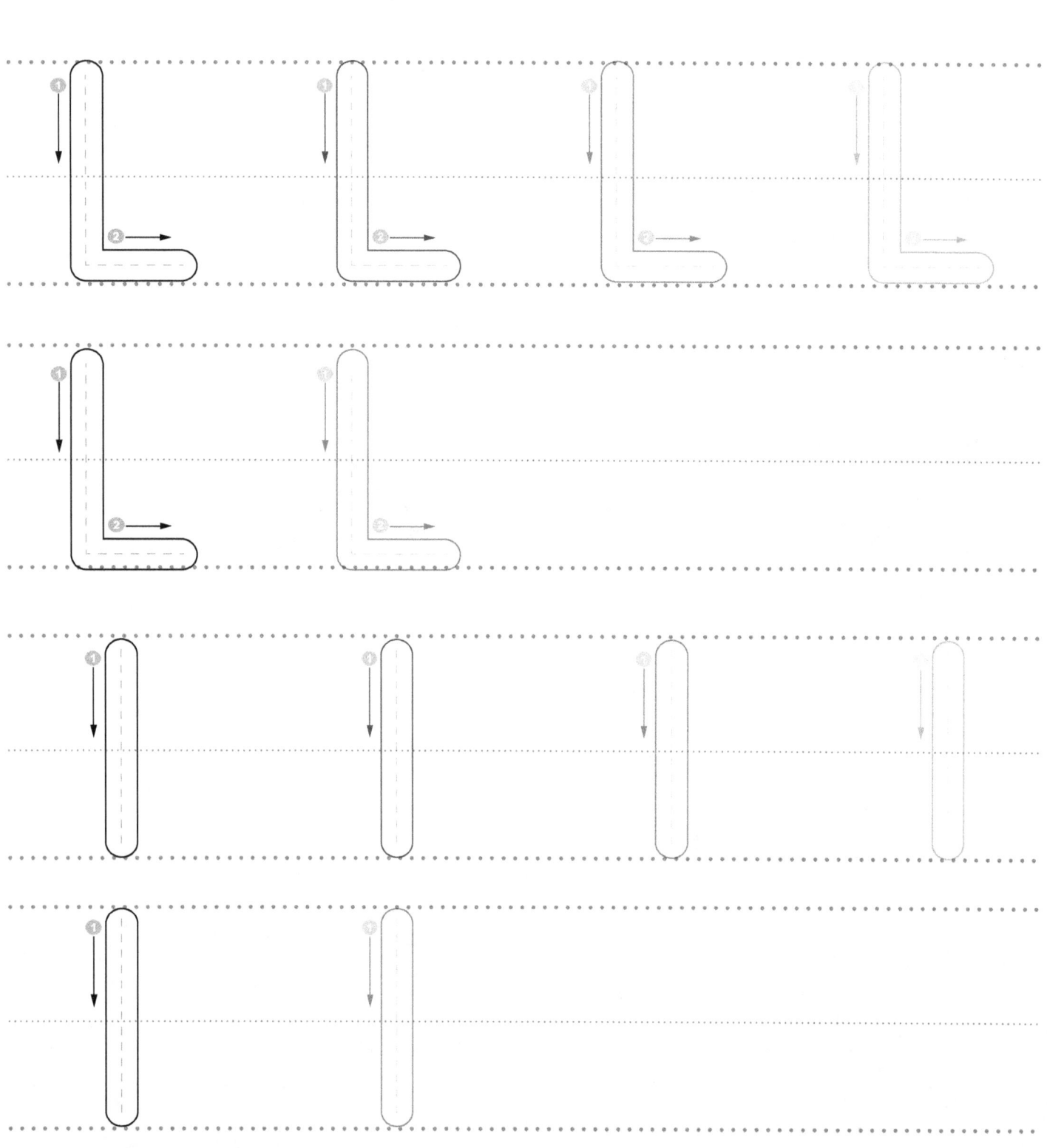

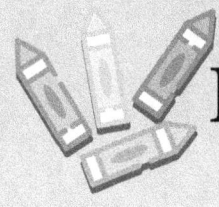 # Find the same letters and color them

Soybeandu

Draw lines to match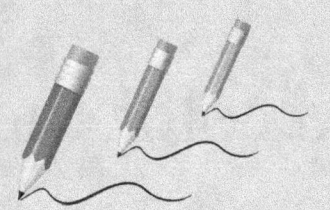

J K L

k l j

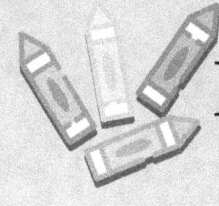 Find the same letters and color them

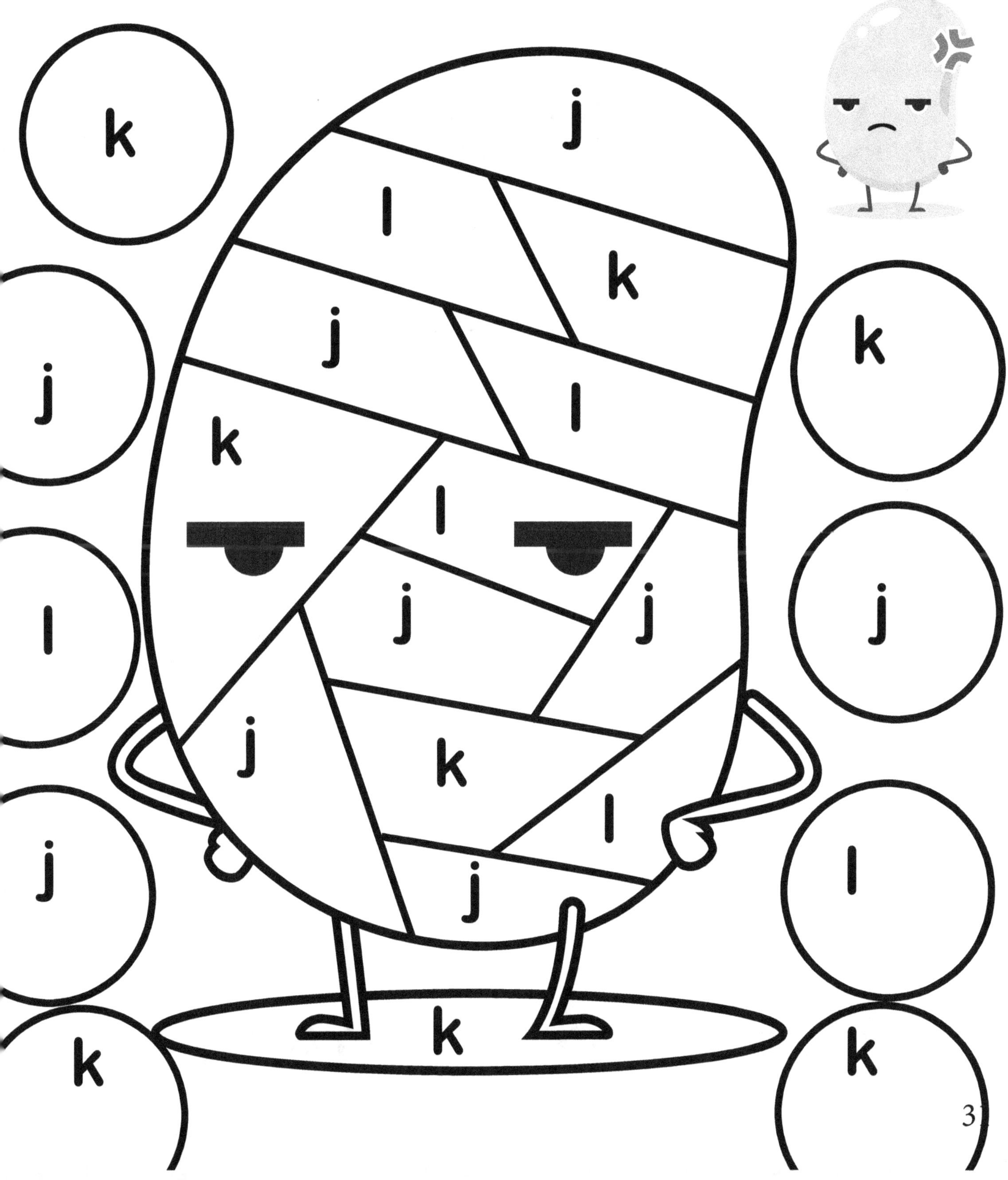

Let's express your

I am cool

I am hungry

I am playful

I am proud

I am okay

feelings with Soybeandu!

I am tired

I am excited

I am loved

I am confident

I am happy

Trace the dotted line and read out loud

Trace the dotted line and read out loud

Trace the dotted line and read out loud

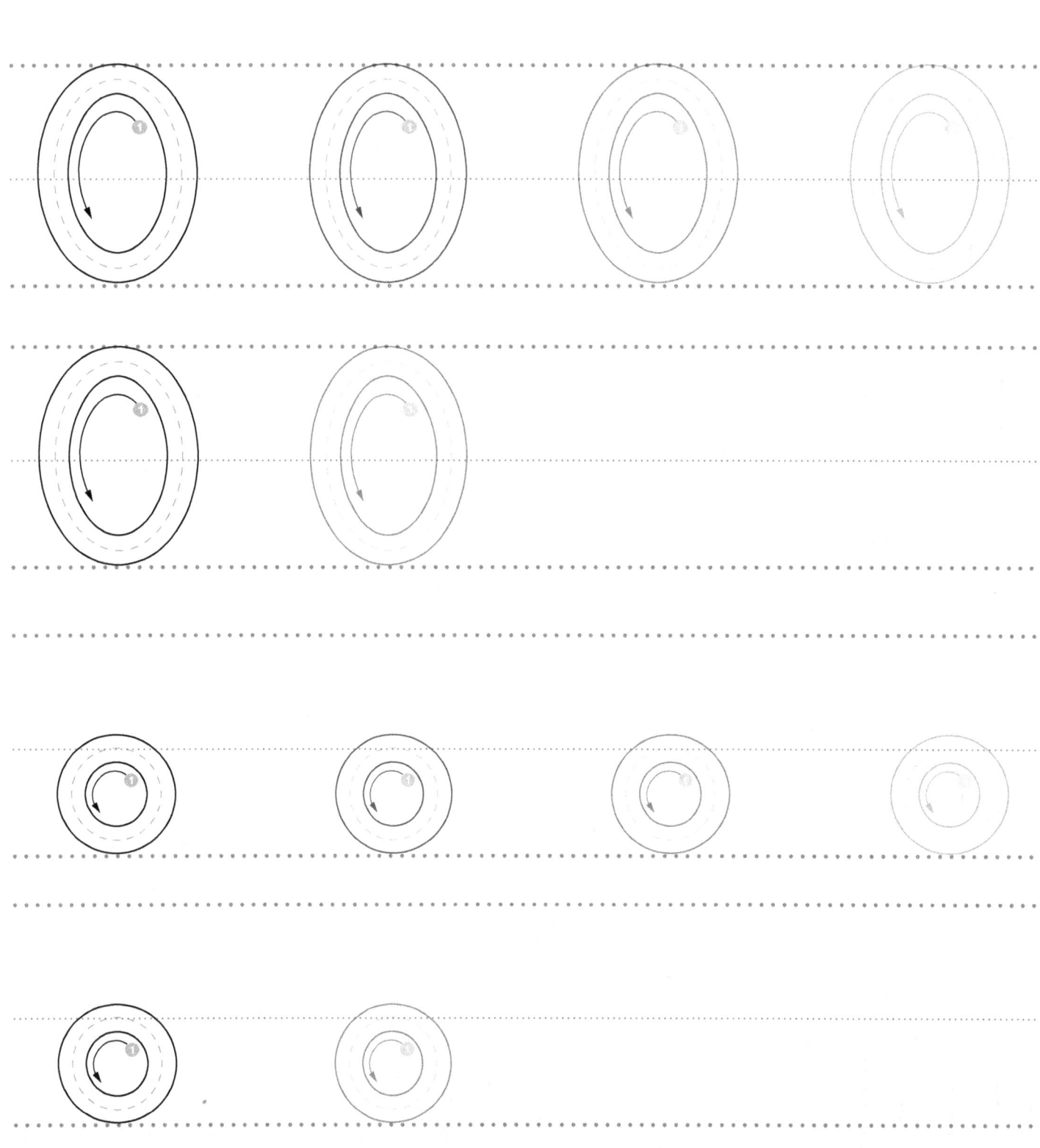

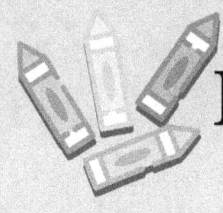 # Find the same letters and color them

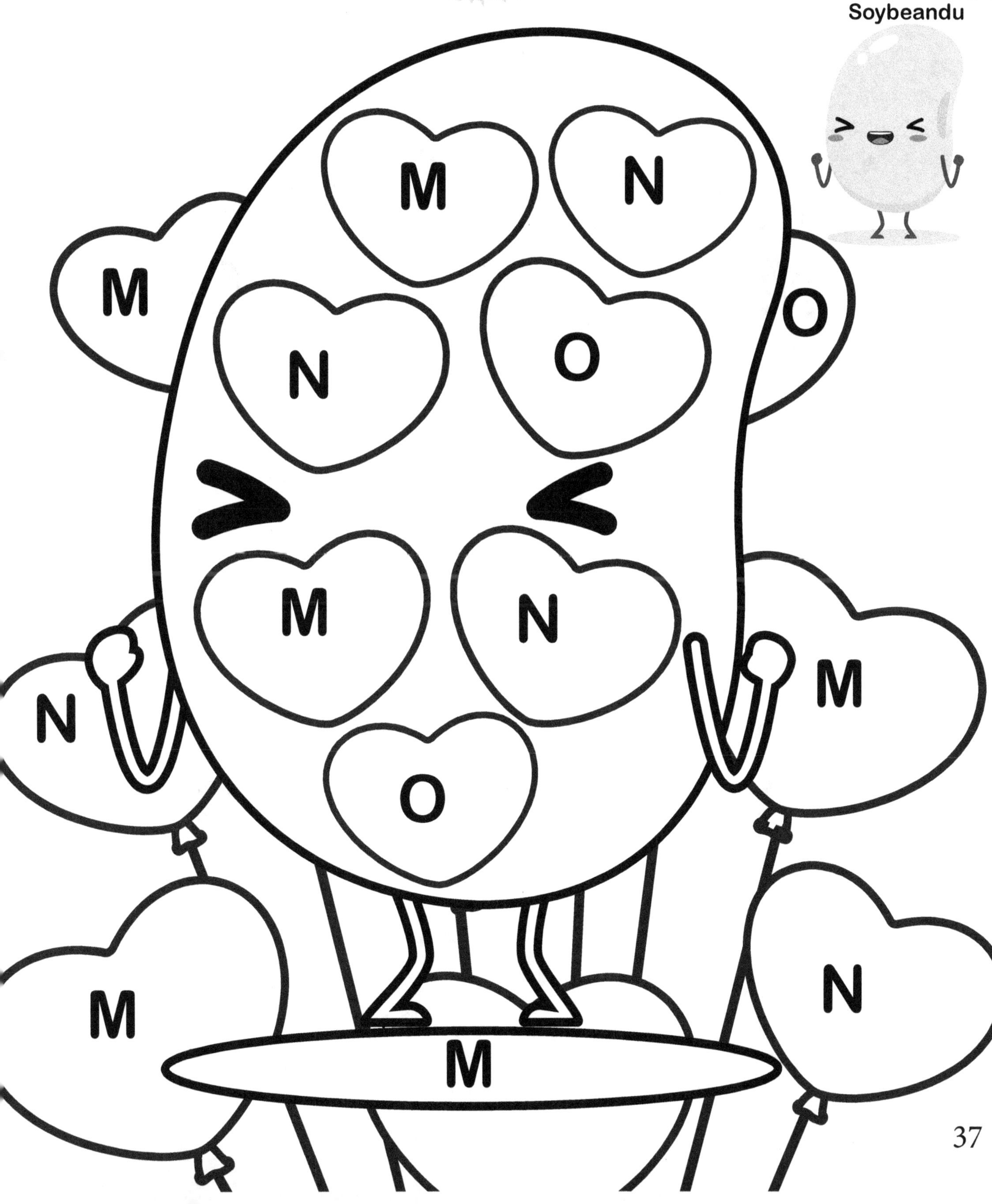

Soybeandu

Draw lines to match

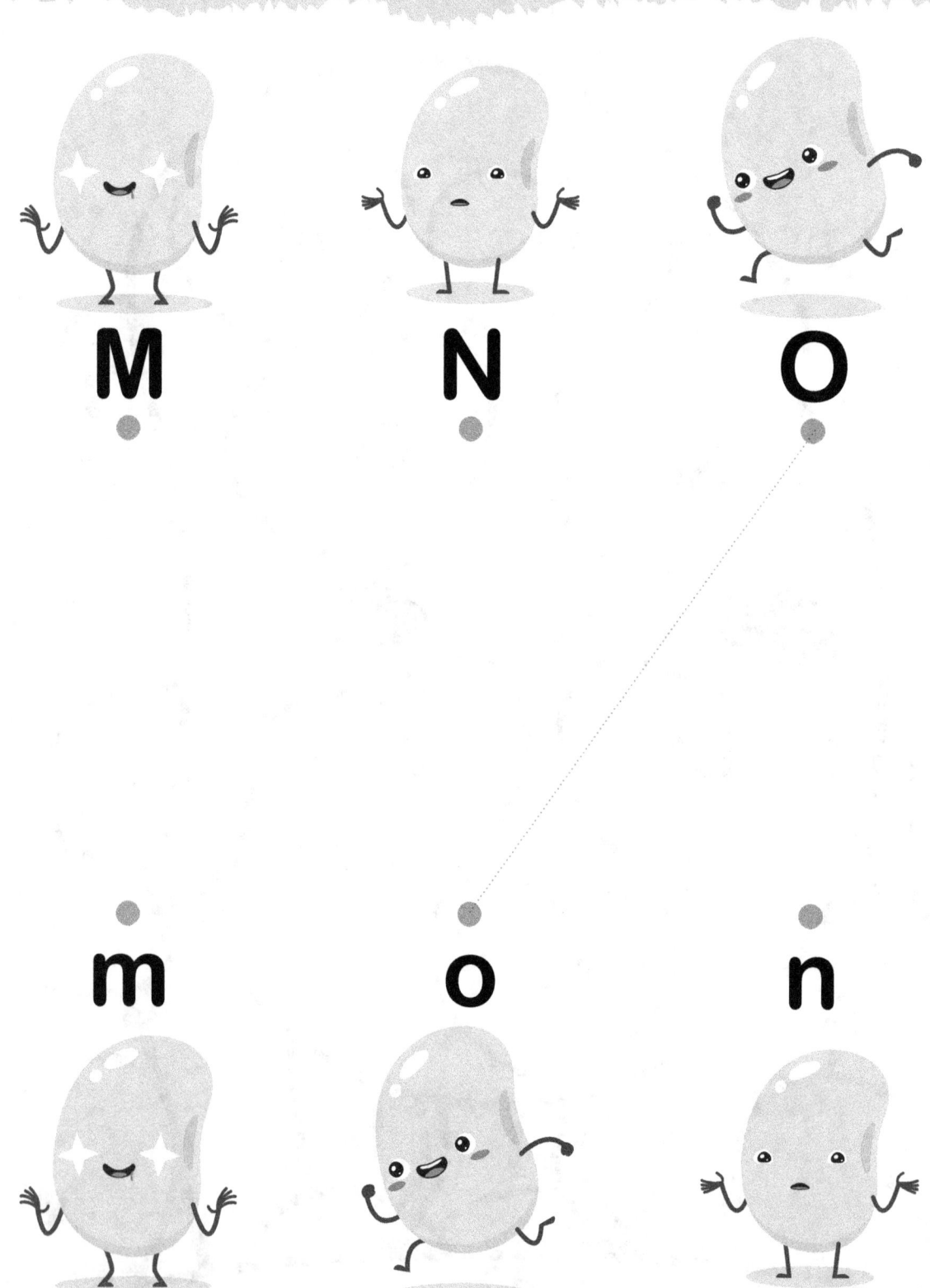

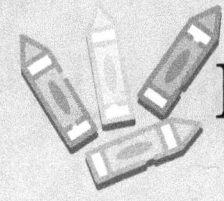 # Find the same letters and color them

Trace the dotted line and read out loud

Trace the dotted line and read out loud

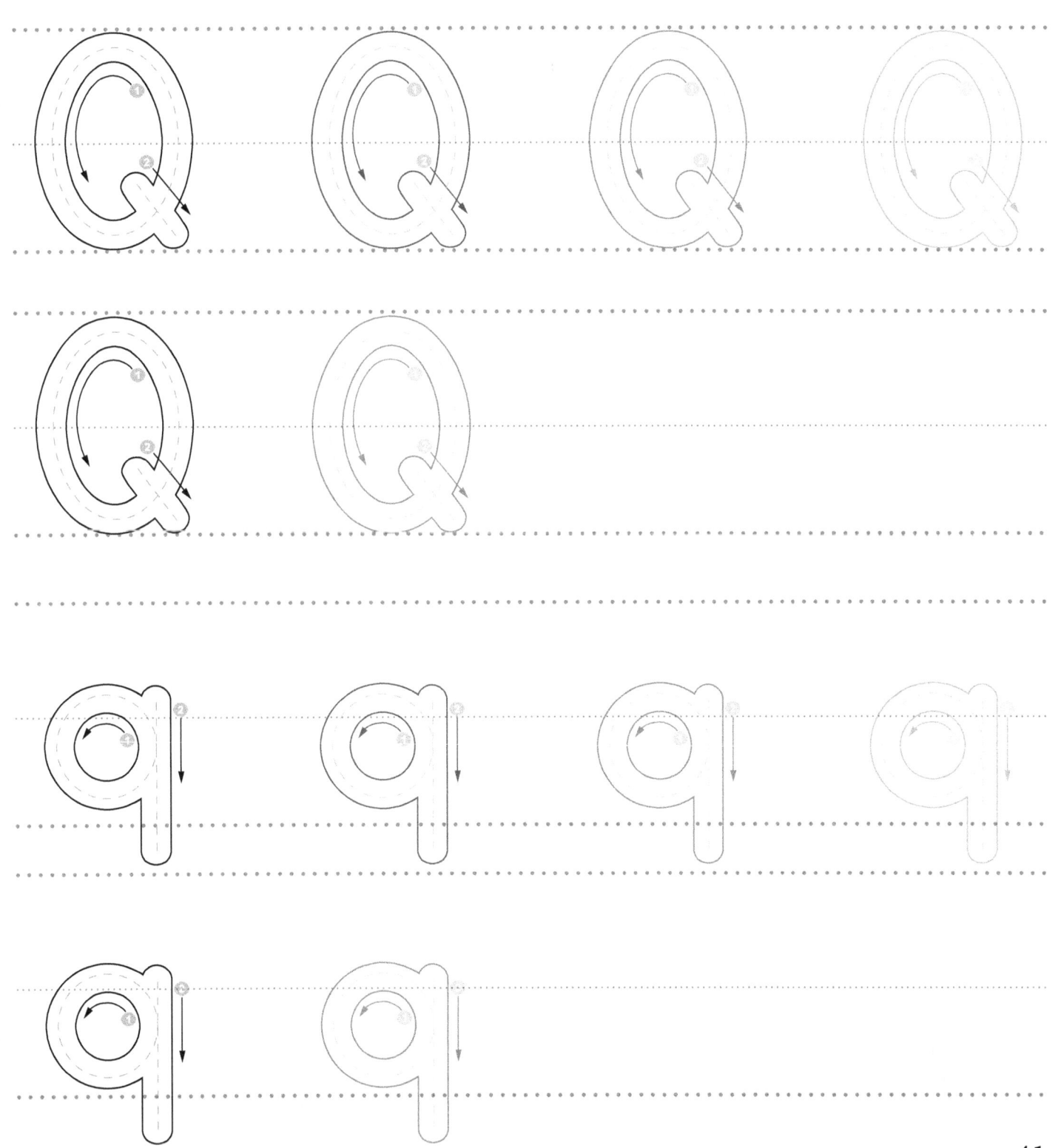

Trace the dotted line and read out loud

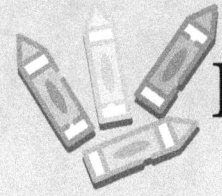 **Find the same letters and color them**

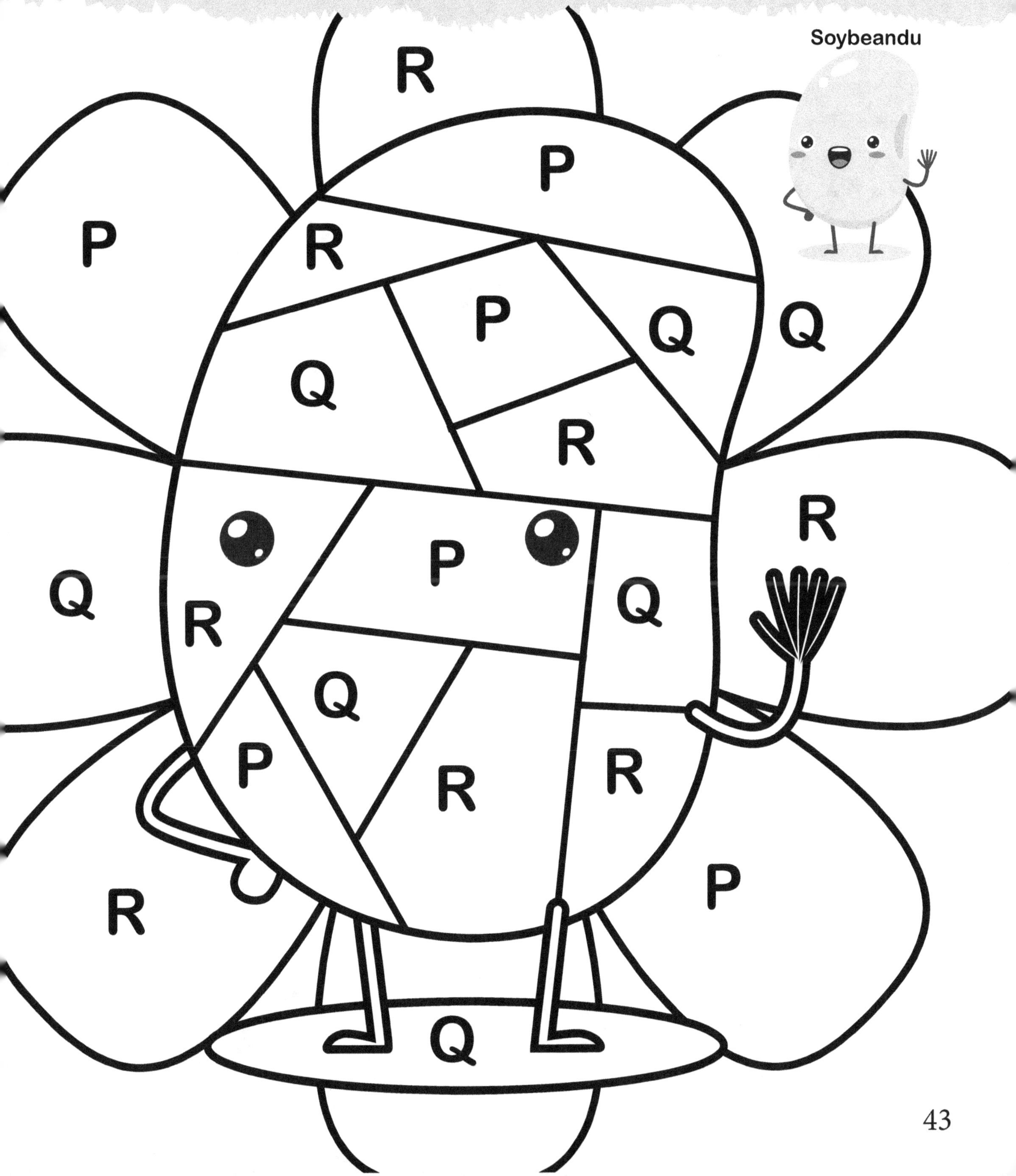

Soybeandu

Draw lines to match

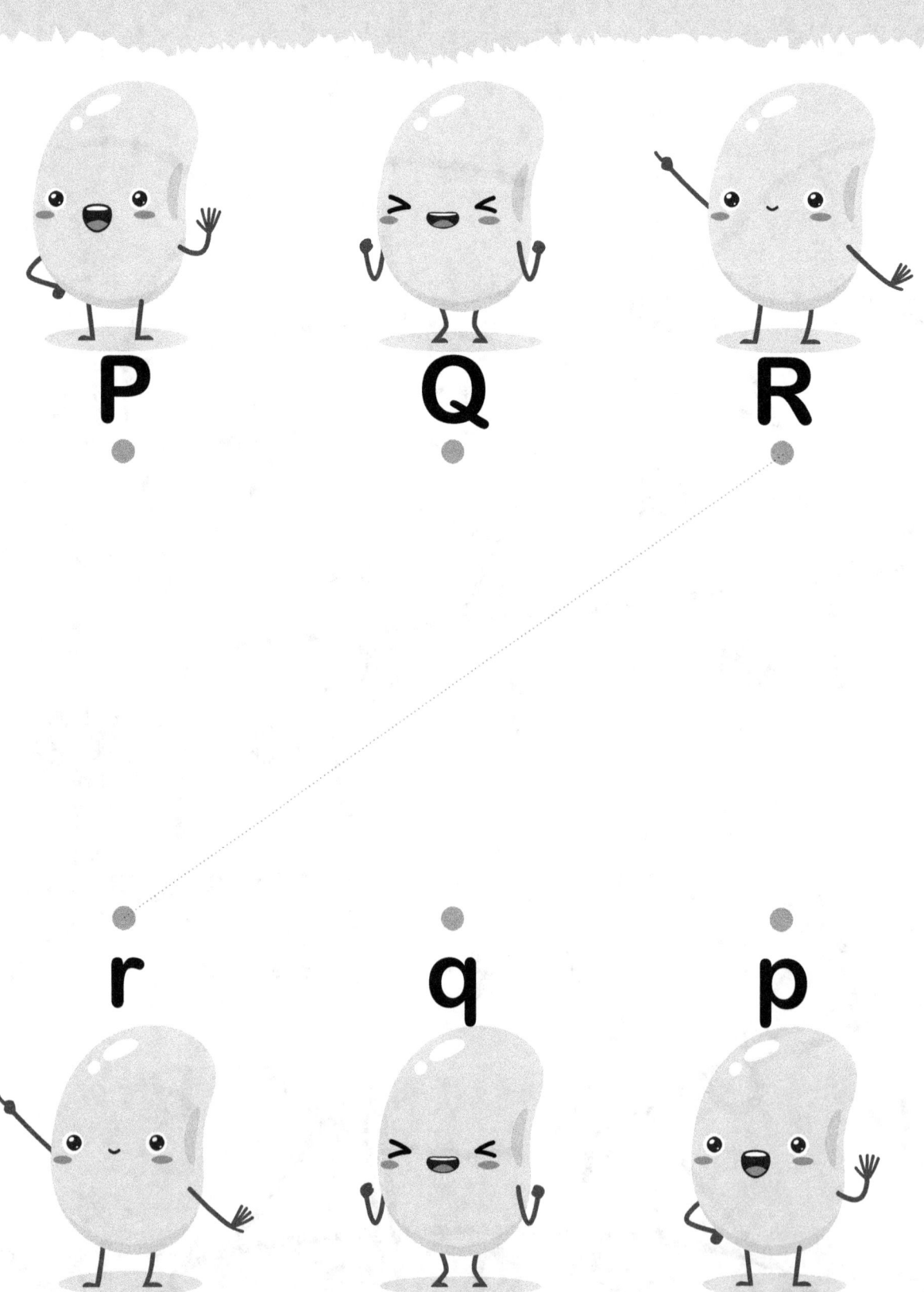

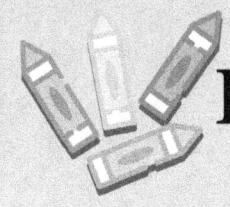 # Find the same letters and color them

Soybeandu

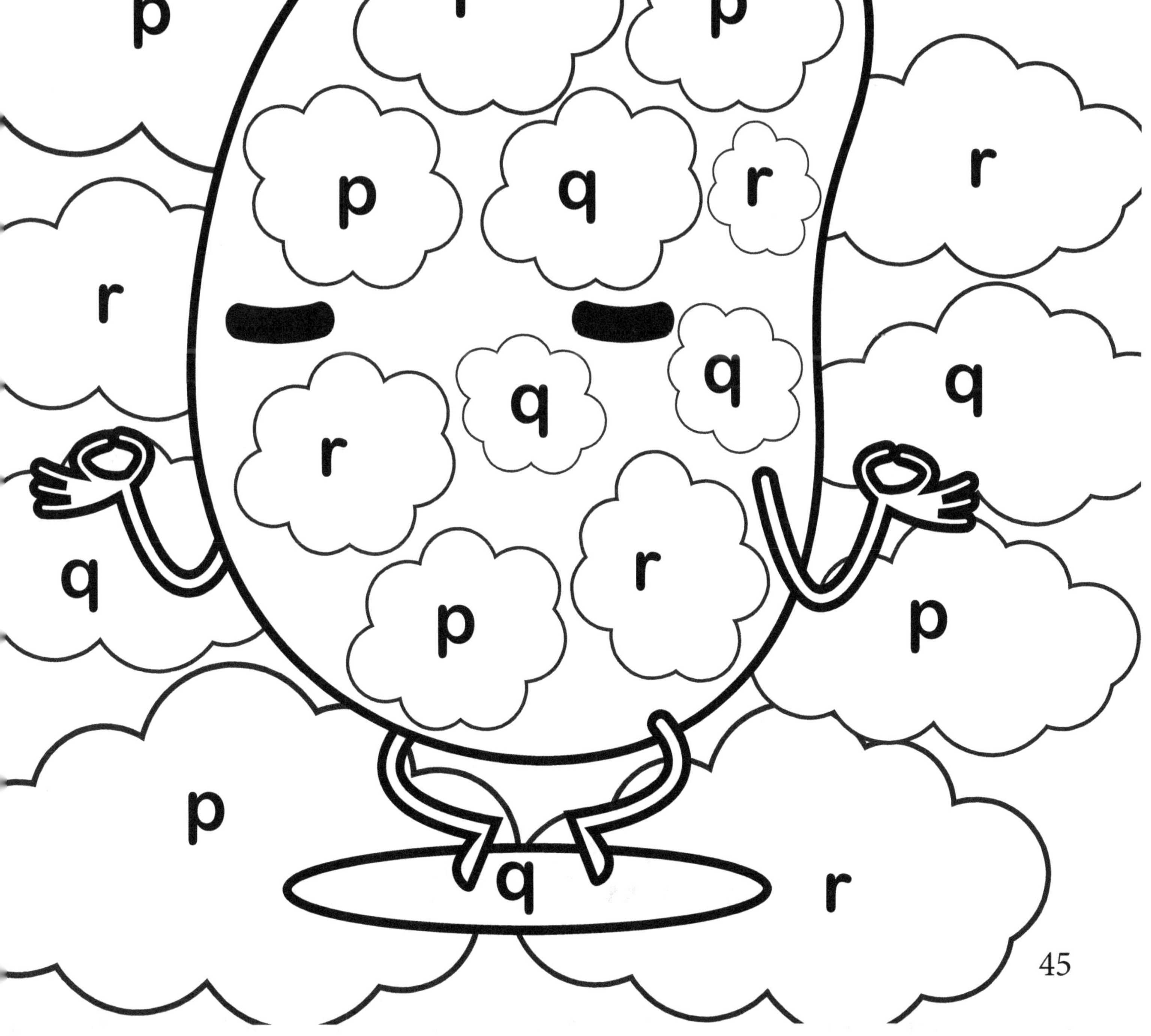

Let's express your

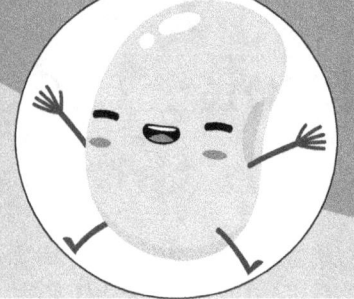

I am sad

I am calm

I am rushing

I am frustrated

I am angry

feelings with Soybeandu!

I am strong

I am embarrased

I am confused

I am shy

I am brave

Trace the dotted line and read out loud

Trace the dotted line and read out loud

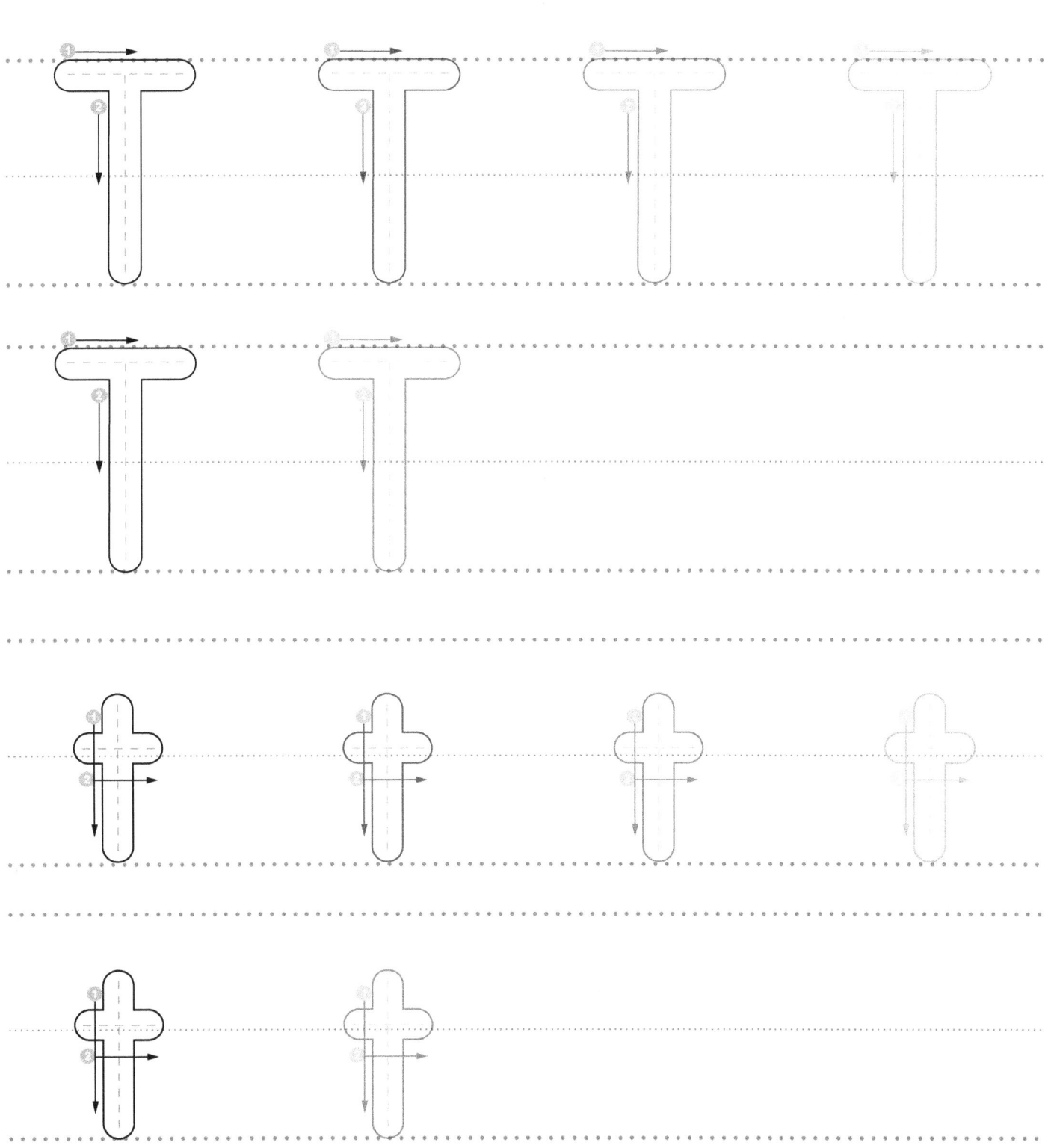

Trace the dotted line and read out loud

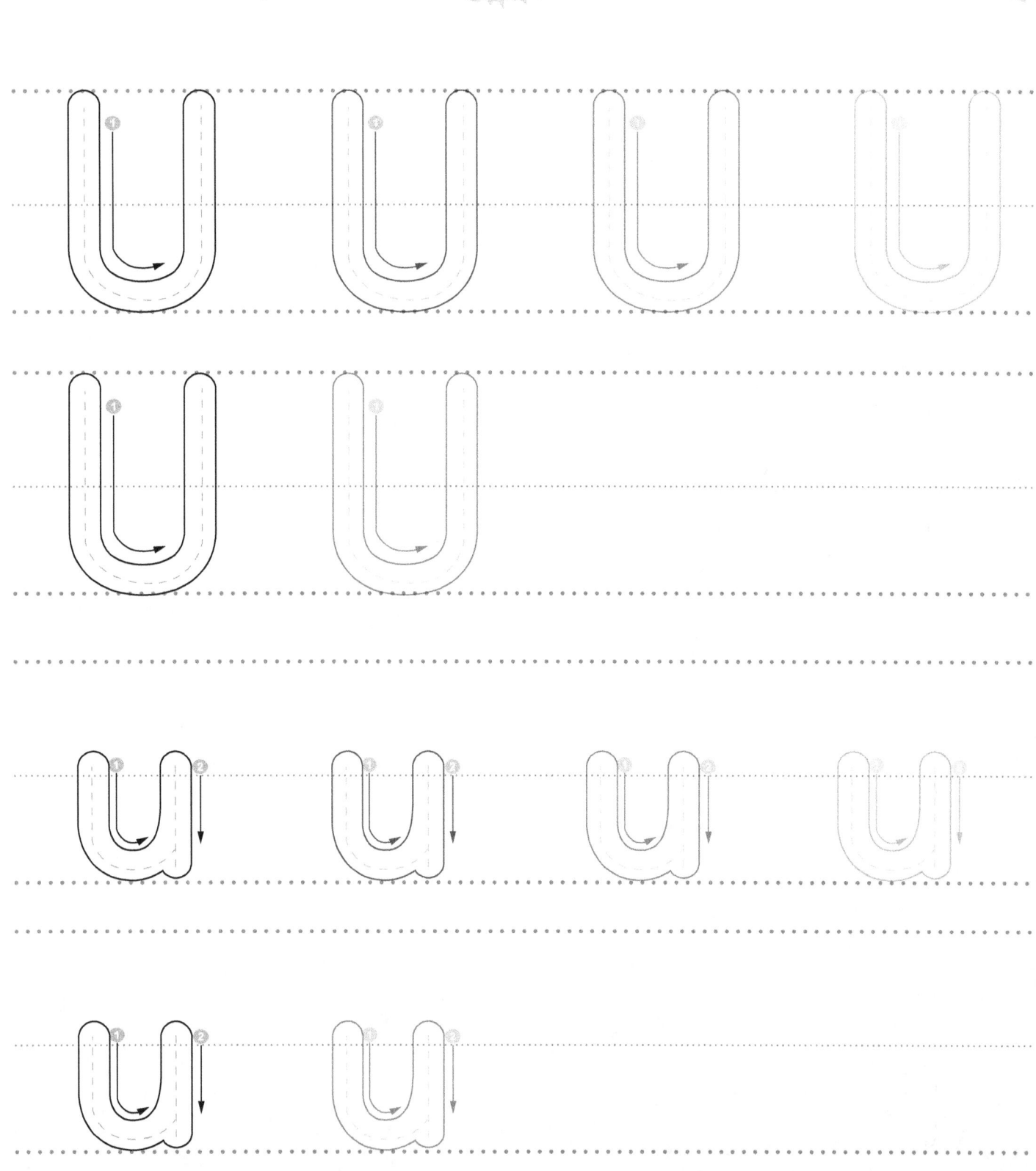

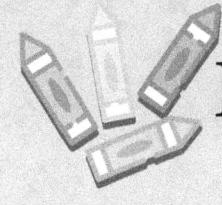 **Find the same letters and color them**

Soybeandu

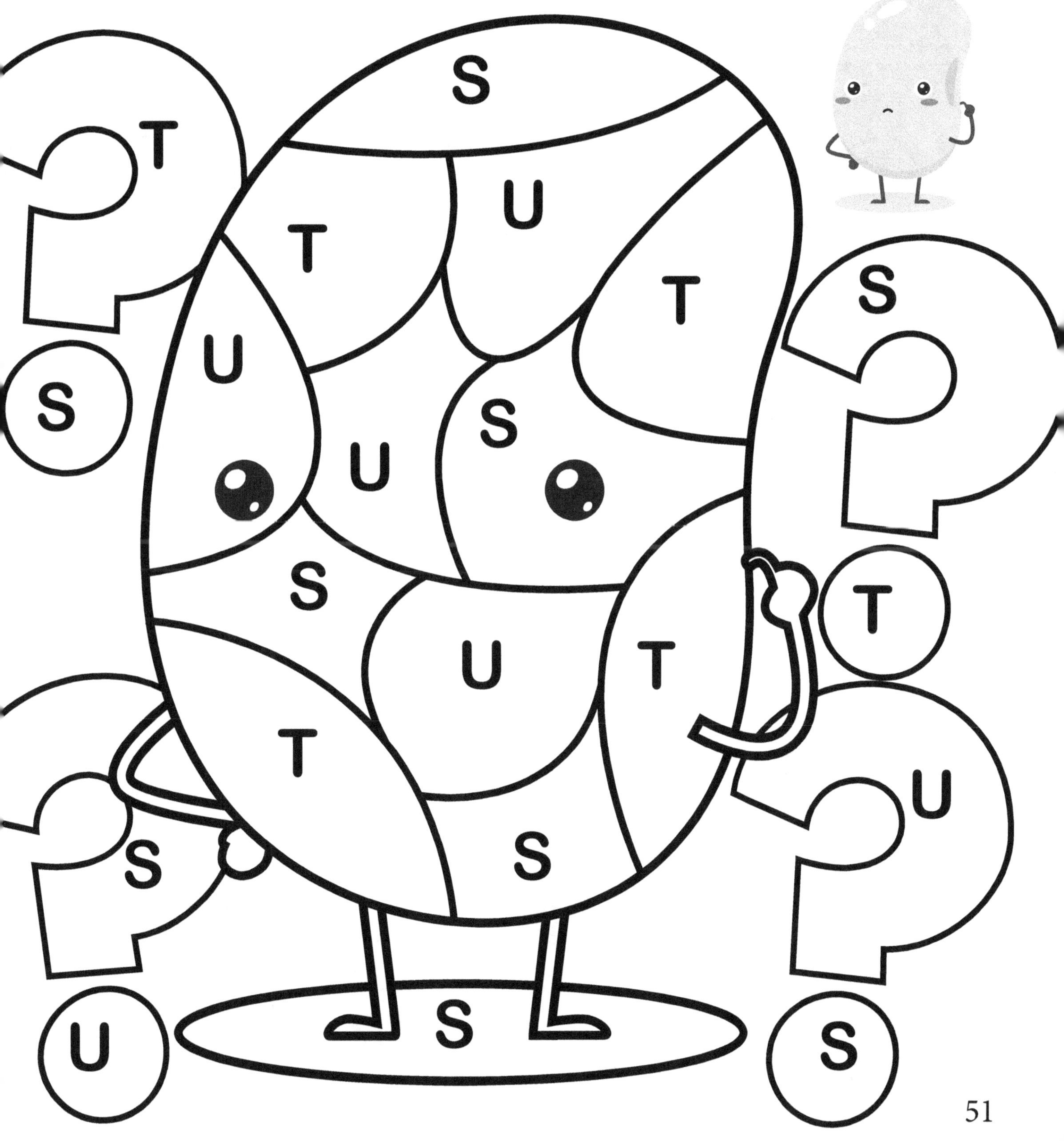

Draw lines to match

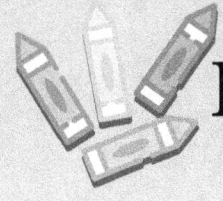 # Find the same letters and color them

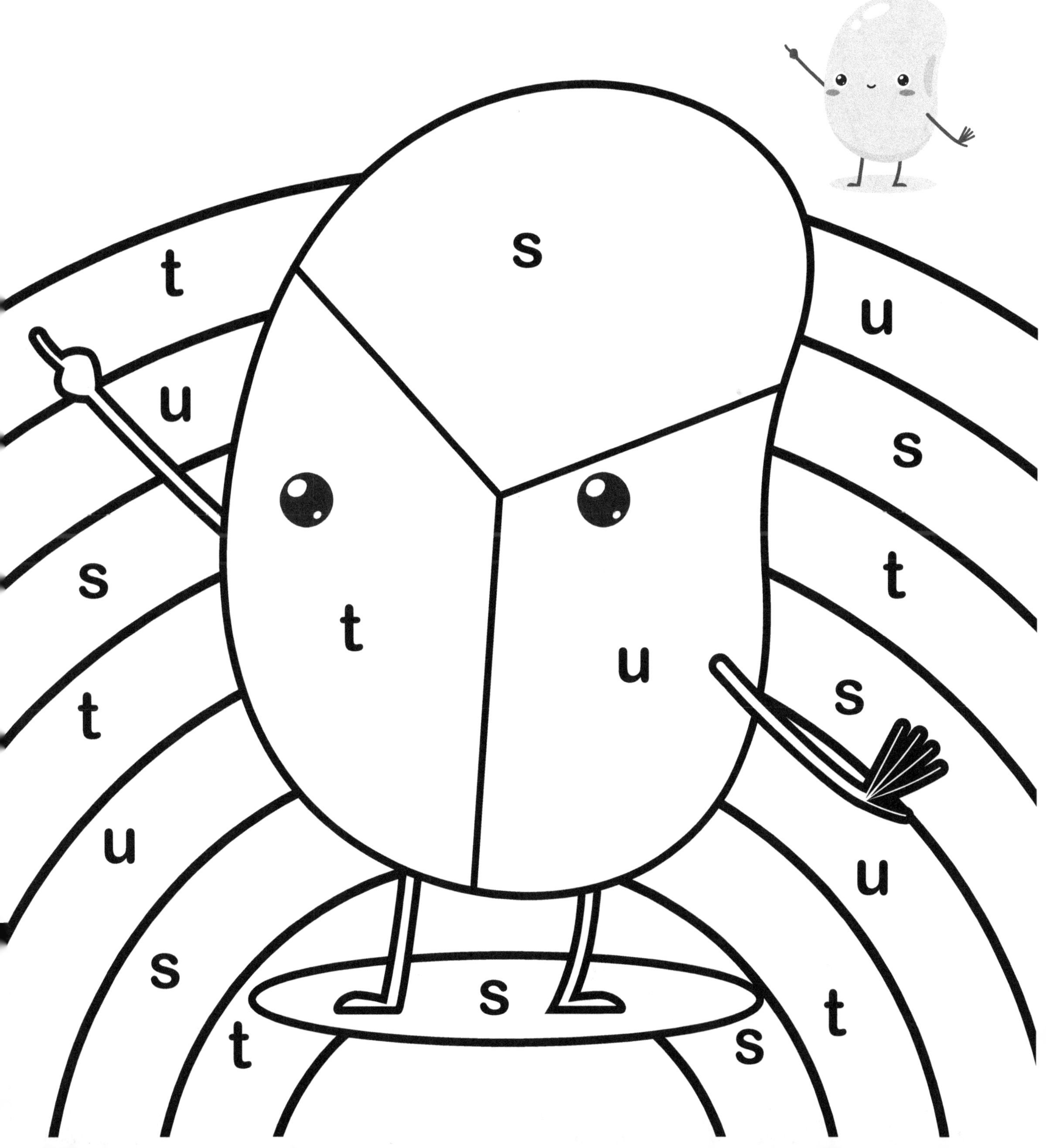

Trace the dotted line and read out loud

Trace the dotted line and read out loud

Trace the dotted line and read out loud

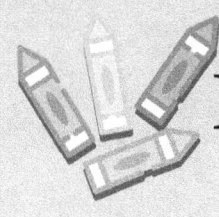 Find the same letters and color them

Soybeandu

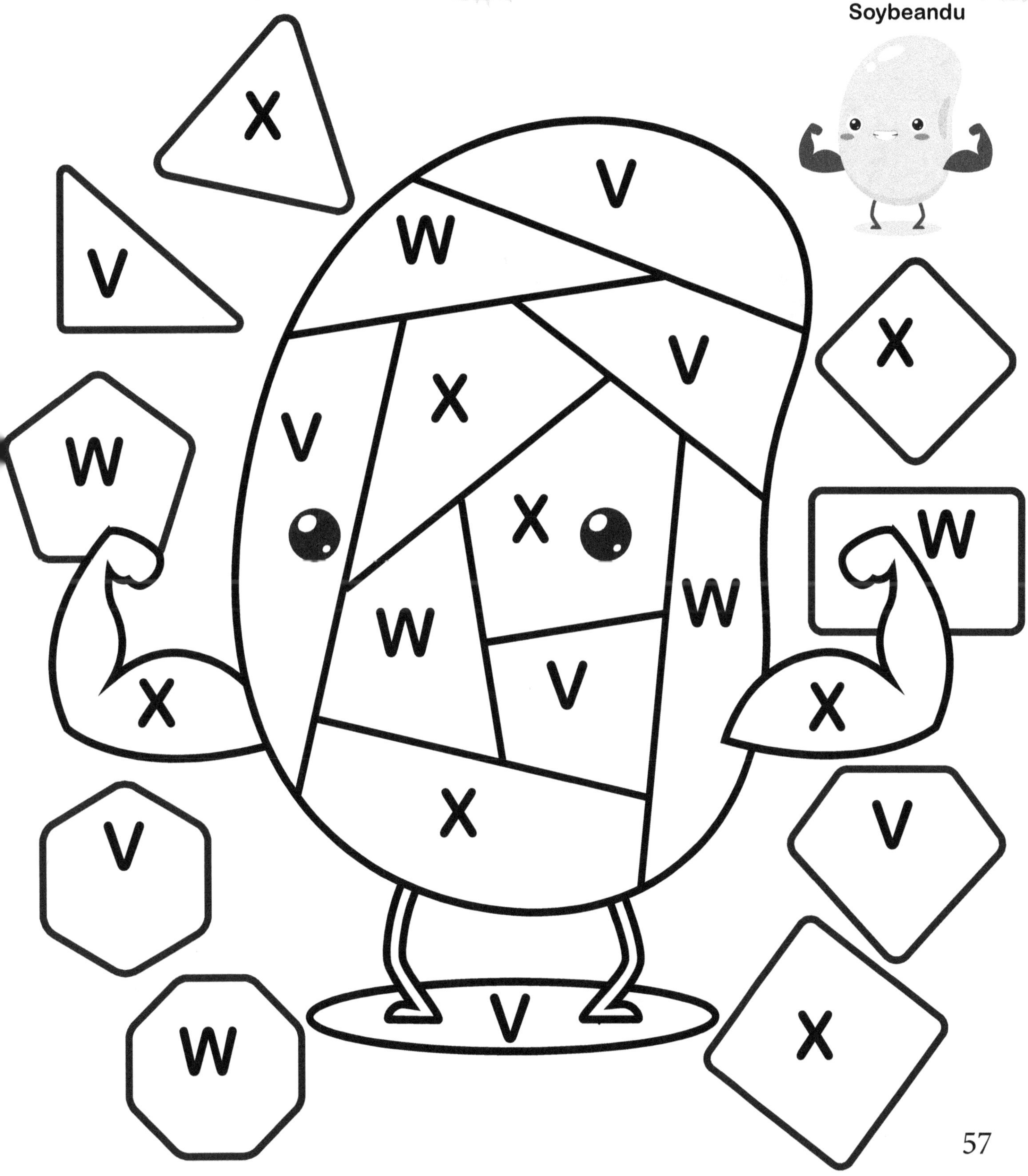

Draw lines to match

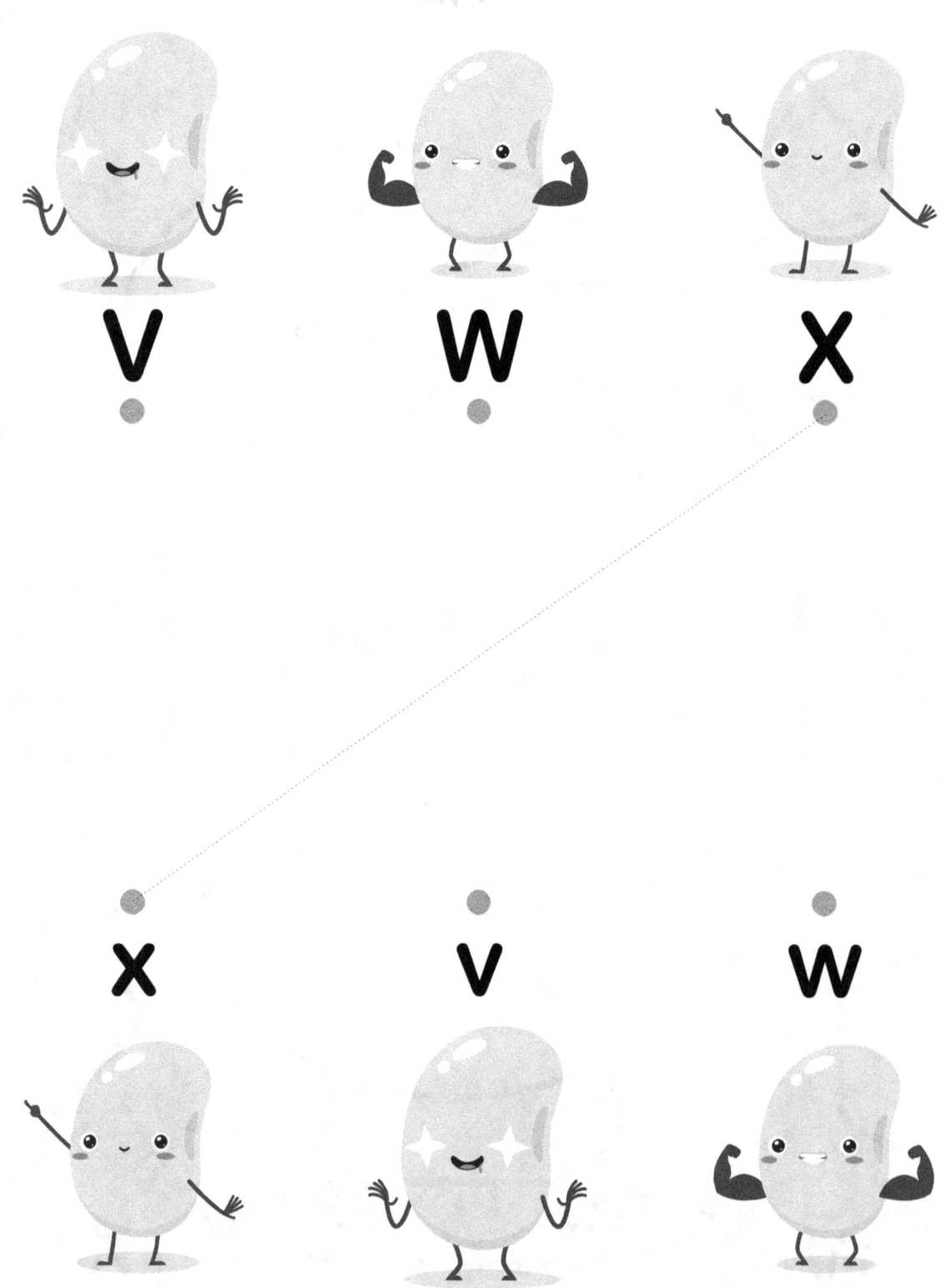

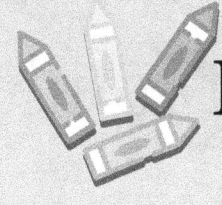 # Find the same letters and color them

Soybeandu

Trace the dotted line and read out loud

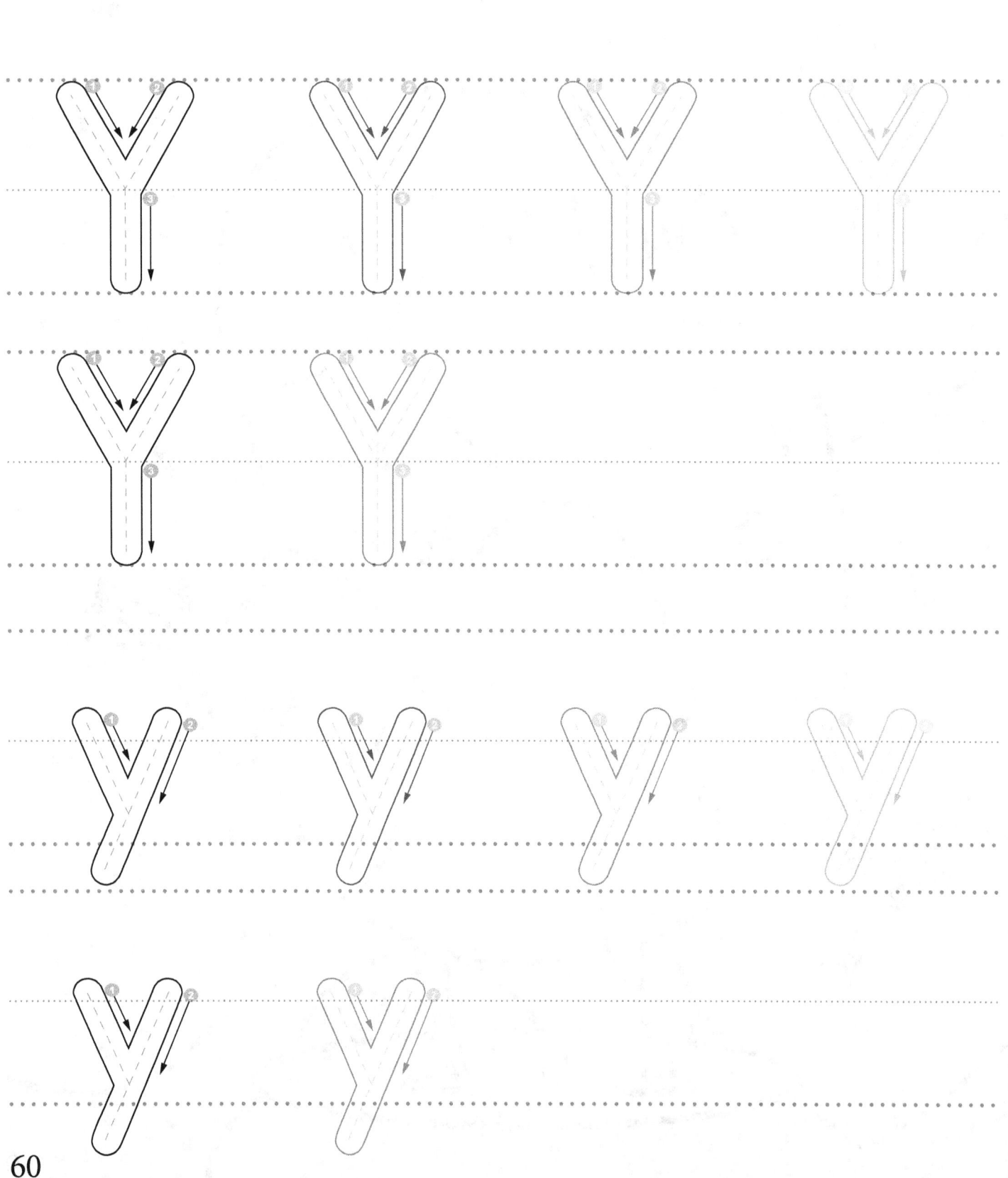

Trace the dotted line and read out loud

Draw lines to match

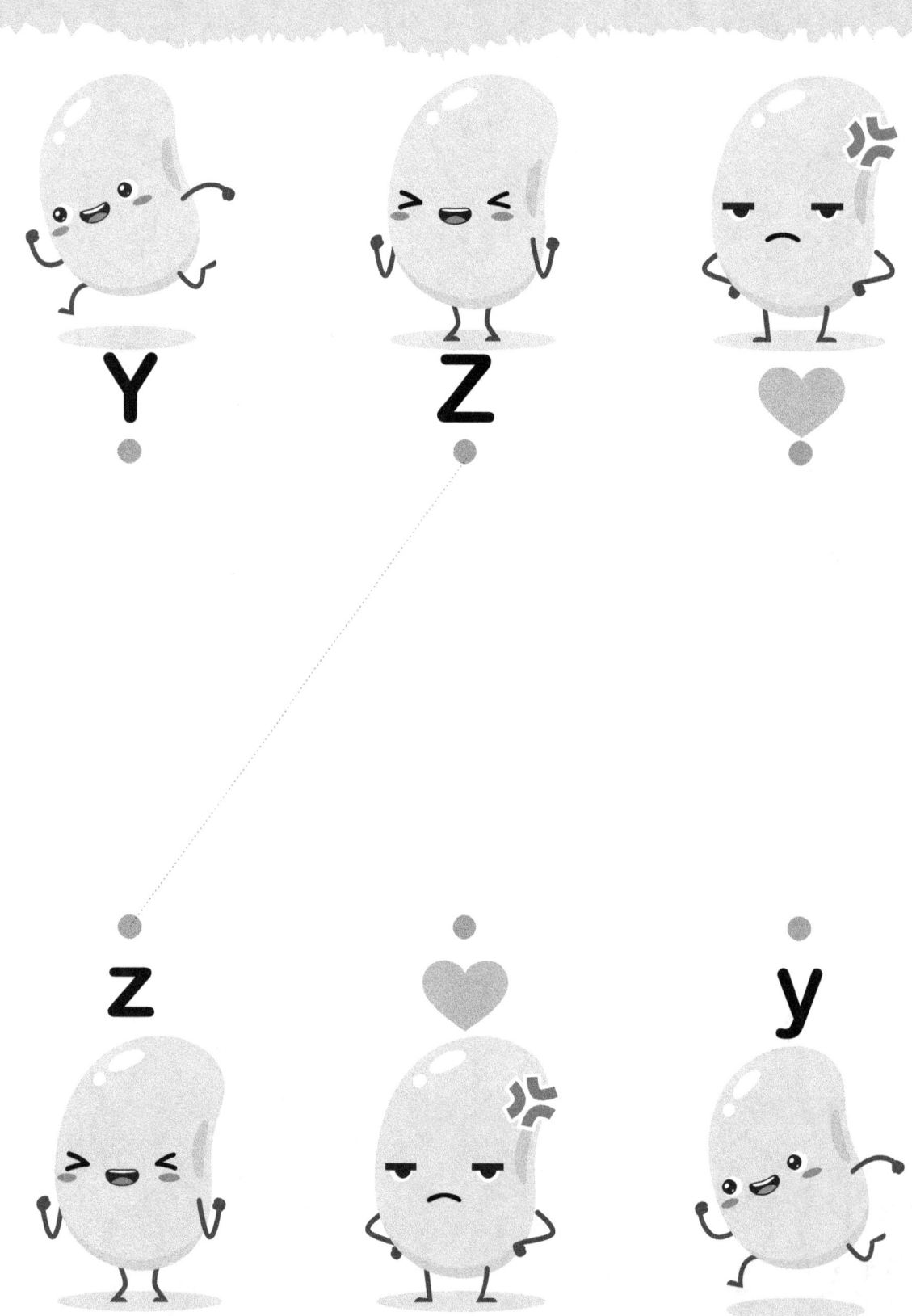

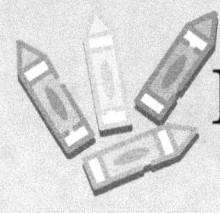 **Find the same letters and color them**

Soybeandu

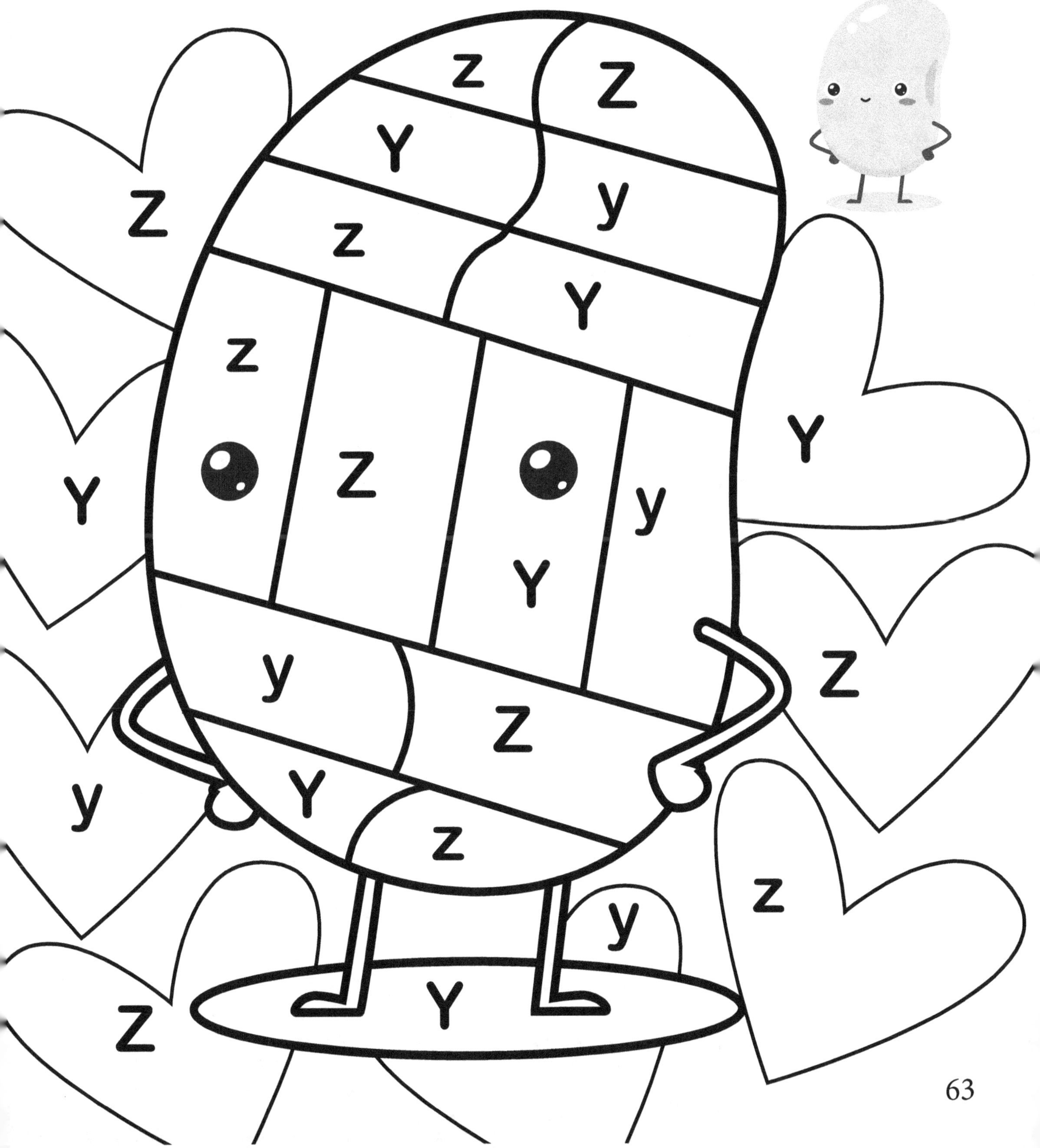

Trace a line from **A** to **Z** and read out loud

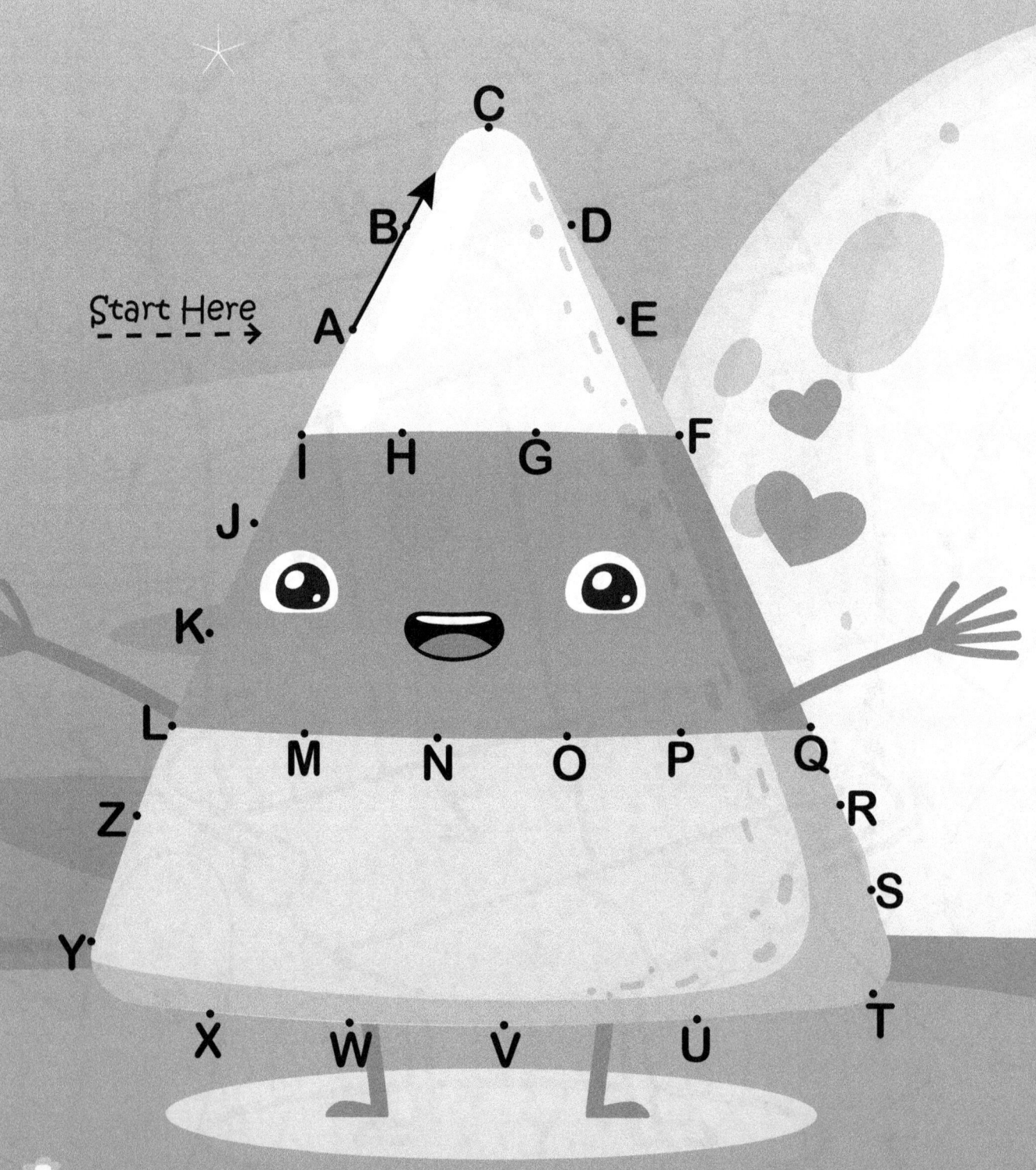

Trace a line from **a** to **z** read out loud

Award

You are amazing!

This award is for

_____ _____
(first name)   (last name)

Great job finishing the book!

Date: _____

Visit Our Website

BigSailorEdu.com

and Get Free & Fun

Educational Material

ABC Workbook Series by Big Sailor Edu

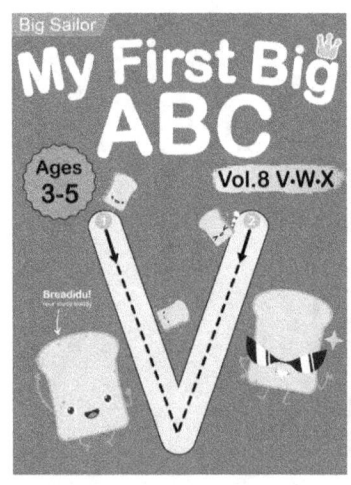

Cambridge Dynasty Press

www.ingramcontent.com/pod-product-compliance
Lightning Source LLC
Chambersburg PA
CBHW081349070526
44578CB00005B/781